SAMUEL JOHNSON
and Biographical Thinking

SAMUEL JOHNSON

and Biographical Thinking

CATHERINE N. PARKE

Missouri Center
for the Book

Missouri Authors
Collection

UNIVERSITY OF MISSOURI PRESS
COLUMBIA AND LONDON

5   4   3   2   1   95   94   93   92   91

Library of Congress Cataloging-in-Publication Data

Parke, Catherine N.
  Samuel Johnson and biographical thinking / Catherine N. Parke.
    p.   cm.
  Includes bibliographical references and index.
  ISBN 0-8262-0789-8
  1. Johnson, Samuel, 1709–1784—Criticism and interpretation.
2. Johnson, Samuel, 1709–1784—Philosophy. 3. Biography (as a
literary form) 4. Biography in literature. 5. Autobiography. I. Title.
PR3537.B54P37   1991
828'.609—dc20   91-12163
                                                          CIP

Designer: Liz Fett
Typesetter: Connell-Zeko Type & Graphics
Printer: Thomson-Shore, Inc.
Binder: Thomson-Shore, Inc.
Typeface: Trump Medieval

For
James, Catherine, Ann, and *Tom*

We know somewhat, and we imagine the rest.

Samuel Johnson, *Life of Roscommon*

Imagination, the art of divining the emotional life of others . . .
is not only commendable inasmuch as it breaks down the
limitations of the ego; it is always an indispensable means of
self-preservation.

Thomas Mann, *Joseph and his Brothers*

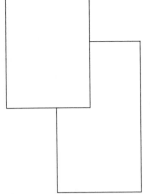

CONTENTS

Acknowledgments   xi

Abbreviations   xiii

Introduction   1

1. Johnson's Mind: The Preface to *The Preceptor* and *The Vision of Theodore*   9

2. Acquaintance and Knowledge: The Prefaces to the *Dictionary* and *The Plays of William Shakespeare*   27

3. Writing in Time: The *Rambler*   53

4. The Conversation of History: *Rasselas*   77

5. The Biography of a Nation: *A Journey to the Western Islands of Scotland*   107

6. Writing Lives: *Lives of the English Poets*   131

Afterword   153

Works Cited   165

Index   175

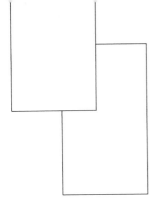

ACKNOWLEDGMENTS

Chapters 4, 5, and 6 are versions of earlier work that appeared in the following essays: "*Rasselas* and the Conversation of History" (in *The Age of Johnson: A Scholarly Annual*); "Johnson, Imlac, and Biographical Thinking" (in *Domestick Privacies: Samuel Johnson and the Art of Biography*); "Love, Accuracy, and the Power of an Object: Finding the Conclusion in *A Journey to the Western Islands*" (in *Biography: An Interdisciplinary Quarterly*, © copyright 1980 by the Biographical Research Center); and "Imlac and Autobiography" (in *Studies in Eighteenth-Century Culture*, © 1977 by the Board of Regents of the University of Wisconsin System).

A 1986 University of Missouri Provost's Research Leave gave me time substantially to draft this book. The English Department provided funds for a graduate assistant, Mary Weaks, who helped check citations. At the University of Missouri Press, my thanks in particular to Beverly Jarrett, Jane Lago, and Loris Mann. For thoughtful readings of the manuscript, encouragement, and hard questions, I owe grateful debts to Paul K. Alkon; W. B. Carnochan; C. Haskell Hinnant; William V. Holtz; Gwin J. Kolb; Catherine N. Parke, Sr.; Richard G. Peterson; Tom Quirk; and Patricia Meyer Spacks. Bill Herbst, Jessie Lawson, and Patricia Whalen contributed their distinctive ways of thinking. My mother, Catherine N. Parke, and my husband, Tom Quirk, must be singled out for special thanks. They contributed to all aspects of this book with Johnsonian generosity. The memory of my father, James H. Parke, provided the forceful example of a lifelong writer. And my daughter, Ann Neal Quirk, brought life abundant.

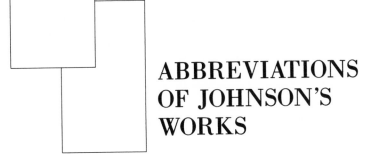

ABBREVIATIONS OF JOHNSON'S WORKS

LP   *Lives of the English Poets.* Edited by G. B. Hill. 3 vols. Oxford: Clarendon Press, 1905.

PD   *Samuel Johnson's Prefaces and Dedications*, by Allen T. Hazen. New Haven: Yale University Press, 1937.

YJ   *The Yale Edition of the Works of Samuel Johnson.* New Haven: Yale University Press, 1958–.

Citations from the Preface to the *Dictionary* are taken from vol. 1 of the AMS reprint of the 1755 edition. 2 vols. New York: AMS Press, 1967.

SAMUEL JOHNSON
and Biographical Thinking

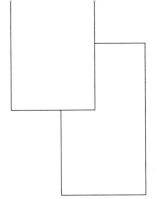

INTRODUCTION

Samuel Johnson's interest in biography, as Donald A. Stauffer remarked in *The Art of Biography in Eighteenth Century England* (1941), "was extraordinary, even for the eighteenth century. He talked biography, thought biography, and to an extent which is often forgotten, wrote biography."[1] Fifty years later Stauffer's observation remains one of the most succinctly accurate and suggestive comments about Johnson and biography. The intervening years of scholarship and criticism have contributed toward remedying the forgetfulness that he identified. Surely none of us is now in danger of forgetting that Johnson wrote biography, which puts us back in good company with his contemporaries for whom the man's biographical writings were among his most popular and important. But how Johnson may have "thought biography" and the dimensions of the man and his mind suggested by these words have yet to be fully appreciated and examined.

My aim in this study is to consider Johnson and biography by examining chronologically a substantial portion of his writings from a perspective that I call *biographical thinking*. This term directs attention to a complex of philosophical and stylistic maneuvers characteristic of his entire body of work, not just the writings that are generically biographical. It names the way his interest in biography goes beyond, while it also includes, an interest in the genre as such. There is substantially more to be gained from this approach than the mere circular pleasure of identifying and then discovering biographical thinking as the principal condition of his

1. *The Art of Biography in Eighteenth Century England*, 395.

work. Rather, such a notion offers a crucial perspective from which new insights may be gained into his distinctive modes of self-empowerment, the characteristic attitudes he strikes, and the postures he assumes. My inquiry will, in part, examine how Johnson came increasingly to understand biography to be for both reader and writer an essential way of experiencing and understanding the world.[2] By the end of his life he had come to see such biographical thinking as our principal means of learning, of sizing up situations, of formulating and solving problems, as in short, basic equipment for living.

To some degree the term biographical thinking overlaps with two more familiar terms: intuition and identification. It names a conventional but nonetheless subtle and intricate mode of understanding that human beings may use with greater or lesser skill but rarely consider consciously. But as this term's meaning accumulates throughout the pages that follow, it will distinguish itself from the activities of intuition and identification while also encompassing them. To engage in biographical thinking is, in a word, to educate oneself over a lifetime in imagining other people's lives and minds. Such imagining is less directed toward certainty than toward the probabilistic enlargement of the horizons of one's sympathies, intelligence, and experience in the presence of others in order to avoid becoming too narrowly, hopelessly, merely ourselves.

As an inquiry into the centrality of biography in Johnson's thinking, arguably his most original and creative habit of mind, my essay also and perhaps more largely examines his theory and practice of education. Thus while I will offer readings of a number of his prose writings, I do not propose these readings as my sole or even my chief end. This is not a critical study as such, though criticism is part of its method. Each chapter examines one or two works, but these readings are neither exhaustive nor purely formal. Rather I take each as evidence of and evidence for (the two not being synonymous) Johnson's habits of mind.

As perhaps does not go without saying, a study such as this one should not be confused with intellectual biography. It is not concerned, except incidentally, with Johnson's training and education, his reading, the philosophical, religious, and literary influences upon him, or with his relation to the leading intellectual questions

2. Richard Ellmann discusses biography in these terms in *Literary Biography*, 19.

of his own day. It thus is less concerned with his intellect than with his mind—with how he begins an inquiry, with what excites his imagination and motivates his curiosity, with what strategies, maneuvers, and commitments serve to further his interest and satisfy his intelligence. The epigraph to this book from his *Life of Roscommon*, "We know somewhat, and we imagine the rest," epitomizes the main interest of my book and its chief proposition about Johnson's mind. I will examine how he negotiated between these two kinds of knowledge, my chief emphasis falling on how, when he *knew somewhat*, he then went about *imagining the rest*. This latter emphasis became, increasingly over the years, Johnson's own. He grew more interested in the mysteries of creativity, of action, of how people came to do what they ultimately did, on the one hand, and less satisfied with explanations invoking the power of circumstance and with causal models of human development, on the other.

The last two generations of Johnsonian critics and scholars have worked to remedy, in particular, the imbalance between Johnson "the man who is dear to us," as Sir Walter Raleigh observed in 1912, the man who was an author "almost by accident,"[3] and Johnson the writer. It may now be time to consider what can be gained from experimenting with valuing *Samuel Johnson* once again, even perhaps valuing him and his ways of thinking *over*, in a self-consciously methodological sense, his writings. This study makes, at least implicitly, a case for what may be gained by such revision. But if I invoke to some degree this past reading of Johnson as interesting largely in and for himself, I do so necessarily in light of the intervening revaluing of him for his writing.[4] The history of the readings of an author make a tacit argument for the postmodern perspective being an aspect of history itself, not merely a critical method. Past readings can never be eliminated or merely reversed. If there ever existed one Samuel Johnson, there certainly is no single figure now. In making new uses of old readings of him, I undertake a practice of which he approved and was himself a master.

Johnson argues the validity of this revision in his kindred com-

3. Cited in Ian Watt's "Dr. Johnson and the Literature of Experience," 15.
4. While my study and Philip Davis's *In Mind of Johnson: A Study of Johnson the Rambler* may share some similar impulses, they differ significantly in that Davis inquires into the Johnson that was, asking what "it meant to be Johnson" and "what being Johnson stood for" (5). My emphasis falls on the Johnson that is.

ments on the difficult and disappointing history of the texts of Shakespeare's plays and the light they shed on the poet's critical intelligence:

> That which must happen to all, has happened to Shakespeare, by accident and time; and more than has been suffered by any other writer since the use of types, has been suffered by him through his own negligence of fame, or perhaps by that superiority of mind, which despised its own performances, when it compared them with its powers, and judged those works unworthy to be preserved, which the criticks of following ages were to contend for the fame of restoring and explaining. (YJ 7:112)

Precisely because Shakespeare had a superior mind, so Johnson speculates, he was probably his own most severe critic. He was more severe than anyone else either would or could have been in taking the measure of his own accomplishments. When the poet evaluated his work, he found it lacking. The tendency to perceive its own deficiency characterizes the gifted mind.

As Johnson analyzed Shakespeare, so he analyzed himself. Indeed because he thought in such ways about himself, he was predisposed to perceive these traits in other writers. Knowing the ins and outs of the gifted mind, he knew how those who accomplish great things inevitably demonstrate thereby that they could have done more. In the Preface to the *Dictionary* he approaches the same subject from a different angle: "To have attempted much is always laudable, even when the enterprize is above the strength that undertakes it: To rest below his own aim is incident to every one whose fancy is active, and whose views are comprehensive; nor is any man satisfied with himself because he has done much, but because he can conceive little." Johnson entertains the possibility for himself that he has greater capacities than he has yet used and is essentially more than he has written. He entertains such a possibility not simply for the purpose of extenuating and apologizing for his failures, though he recognizes these to be reasonable ploys for any writer, but chiefly in order to make readers sensitive to measuring such discrepancies within themselves.

The other side of the disappointment of perceiving how performance rarely embodies our full powers is the hope of newly perceiving the full measure of our as yet untapped resources of creativity. Disappointment and hope, failure and possibility are always reciprocal. Such bifocal perception maintains us in a healthy state of perennial alertness and dissatisfaction. While Johnson identified the human condition as essentially characterized by dissatisfaction which, in turn, regularly deludes and undermines our possibilities, so he recognized that precisely this same dissatisfaction, if properly organized, stimulates creative powers and hope.

The foregoing remarks combine to depict two of the dominant characteristics of Johnson's behavior as writer: his belief that his readers are real and his sense of responsibility to act on this belief. Such notions may seem to be a minimal requirement for any writer, though they are probably no more common among writers than among people in general. In a distinctly American rendering of a Johnsonian idea, Ralph Waldo Emerson once noted this deficiency and its remedy when he exhorted his readers to "be poised, and wise, and our own, to-day. Let us treat the men and women well; treat them as if they were real; perhaps they are."[5] The reality of other people, or more precisely, our responsibility to act toward others "as if" they were real was for Emerson, as for Johnson, the foremost ethical principle. It invokes the imagination to forward the actions of the soul. The assumption and the literary behavior that accompany and dramatize such acts of mind constitute Johnson's biographical thinking.

While this book takes Johnson and a representative sample of his prose writings selected from throughout his career as its subject matter, it also considers how the man and his work serve as an occasion for certain kinds of thinking on our part. When brought into the orbit of his own deep and abiding interest in biography, my thinking will at best, in some fashion, imitate his. All criticism is, to some degree, modeled on formal imitation. Johnson conceived of his poems *London* and *The Vanity of Human Wishes* as being true to Juvenal. But he also conceived of them as being true to, which is to say communicative with, his own age. He would never have doubted that he made, rather than in some naive sense found, a meaning for his contemporaries in the works of a writer, such as Juvenal, distant and long dead. Meaning can occur only in the present, but it is not thereby one-sided. It must be a conversation with the past, not a soliloquy.

For these reasons Johnson will sometimes be in center focus as this study's object of investigation, while at other times he will be either the director or the direction of our gaze. This study is *of* him and takes its direction *from* him, but it is not always *about* him.

5. "Experience," 60.

Rather, he fills this book in the same distinctive way he filled his writings—by taking on a variety of roles and functions. One of these functions, and perhaps the most troubling for some readers, is his role as interlocutor with a number of modern and contemporary thinkers. Their presence in this book serves not to explicate Johnson anachronistically but to engage him in the kind of conversation he understood to be the only kind possible: a conversation in the present, for the present, and in the present tense.

For readers who hold out the ideal of some pure recovery of the past in its own terms as the only true and appropriate end of literary study, the presence of thinkers such as Sissela Bok and Kenneth Burke may be troubling. Invoking our contemporaries is, however, central to my presuppositions and methods. They do not provide merely illustrative commentary on Johnson but are positively constitutive of an argument about how, in the late twentieth century, he exists as a figure occupying an intellectual space that also includes his successors—Bertrand Russell, Gertrude Stein, Virginia Woolf, William James, Ludwig Wittgenstein, among them. As surely as they owe debts to him, so he owes debts to them. It would be mistaken to think otherwise. The debt, as Jorge Luis Borges once observed in noting how Hawthorne's particular quality has been created or determined by his heir Kafka, "is mutual."[6] There is a healthy inevitability about such anachronistic indebtedness that says something basic about life itself, its forms and forces. The fact that Johnson can still be read and has grown in interest to readers in the second half of this century depends critically upon the family resemblances between his thinking and our own. This study aims to identify these resemblances. To say this is not to value ourselves over Johnson but, to invoke a different metaphor, simply to recognize that by definition a conversation has two sides and that to be on speaking terms with our past is part of what it means to be alive.

Chapter 1, "Johnson's Mind," reads his Preface to *The Preceptor* and *Vision of Theodore* as instances of two distinctive and distinct attitudes toward education that the succeeding chapters will trace in subsequent work. These two attitudes embody his understanding of the double and sometimes divided nature of learning. By half learning is a tentative, tenuous, and vulnerable drama of power that, while it evokes the student's fears and insecurities, also tempts the teacher's appetite for power. By half it is also an experience

6. "Nathaniel Hawthorne," 57.

offering moments of insight, clarity, and creativity. Learning was for Johnson a model of the creative process, the moment of new insight being unpredictable until it occurs and recognizable only after the fact. Collectively such moments invite our acknowledging that the mystery of knowing is inexplicable in causal terms alone. One can, however, prepare to receive and participate in such intuitions that provide the occasion radically to revise our ways of seeing and knowing both ourselves and the world.

Chapter 2, "Acquaintance and Knowledge," examines the genre that Johnson thought he wrote best, the preface. By giving particular attention to the prefaces to the *Dictionary* and *Shakespeare*, this chapter considers the significance of the particular competence he felt in writing this genre and his keen recognition of how important it is to acquaint ourselves with new knowledge before attempting to learn it through rational routes of explanation. He believed that the preface embodies the kind of knowledge we mean when we talk about becoming acquainted with another person, which is to say knowing that person in a multitude of ways we can never fully articulate but which are nonetheless real and important.

In light of the second chapter's model of education by acquaintance, Chapter 3, "Writing in Time," proposes the *Rambler* as an undertaking that unfolds in and defines itself chiefly by and through time, as the *Dictionary*, by contrast, defines itself chiefly in space. I will focus on the distinctive way these essays, as a series, ground their notions of education in the author's commitment to taking his readers seriously by imagining them to be real, which is to say temporal beings. In the *Rambler* Johnson encourages his readers to adopt the strenuous requirement of taking their own lives as seriously as he takes them in preparing essays for their inspection.

In the context of the earlier chapters' development of key principles in his model of education, Chapter 4, "The Conversation of History," examines *Rasselas* as a parable about how teaching and learning are central to human relationships. This fiction compositely dramatizes his insights into psychology and ethics in their intersection with biography. Here education is dramatized as a conversation whose politics center on the characters coming to trust in the uses of difference and repetition in order to ensure their freedom as individuals and to test their responsibility as social beings.

Chapter 5, "The Biography of a Nation," examines how Johnson's emphasis on the function of acquaintance in the genre of the preface also informed his notions about travel literature. His *Jour-*

ney to the Western Islands of Scotland revises the reader's usual expectations about such writing, as do his prefaces, by tipping the balance away from the ideals of analysis and explanation and toward the aims of acquaintance and intelligibility. In so doing he discovered the radically humbling nature of travel writing that takes as its principal aim the attempt to imagine other people's lives as they are conditioned by history and custom. In undertaking to write a cultural and historical biography, Johnson encountered the challenging problems posed by a kind of writing that requires its author simultaneously to pursue knowledge through rational routes of explanation and biographical routes of acquaintance.

Finally in Chapter 6, "Writing Lives," I conclude by examining the *Lives of the English Poets*. Originally entitled *Prefaces, Biographical and Critical, to the Works of the English Poets*, this last project returned Johnson to the form he felt he wrote best, the preface. He imaginatively expands the genre to encompass the thinking he had done about biography over a lifetime. These biographies give evidence of how, at the end of his career, he had come to understand and to write biography as a necessary part of living. As his earlier work prepares us to expect, biography in the *Lives* is not just an instrument but a medium of thought through which we claim a past, live a present, and imagine a future for ourselves.

The inquiry that these chapters cumulatively pursue into Johnson's epistemology, ethics, theories of teaching and learning, and notions of genre unfolds less as a linear incremental exposition than as a gathering of the themes and emphases presented in this introduction. They accumulate into a meditation on a single topic: Samuel Johnson's habits of thought, which are in motivation and design radically biographical. While this study is by no means exhaustive in its consideration of his works, I do attempt to read a substantial representation of his body of writing in order to exemplify and to test my central proposition about Johnson and biography. My choices are, I hope, sufficient both to engage the reader by casting new light on some familiar and some not so familiar Johnsonian texts and to depict his creative consciousness.

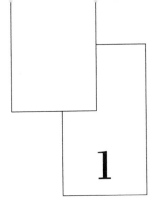

1 JOHNSON'S MIND

The Preface to *The Preceptor* and
The Vision of Theodore

FROM TEACHER TO TEACHING

In April 1748, just over ten years after Johnson had set out for London to try to earn a living by writing, Robert Dodsley published *The Preceptor*, an educational anthology intended for "the Youth of this Nation." This work included two commissioned pieces by Johnson: a preface, addressed to teachers, and an allegory on the dangers and virtues of habits, *The Vision of Theodore, the Hermit of Teneriffe, Found in his Cell*, addressed to students. Dodsley's commission of Johnson had its circumstantial ironies. Before he left for London in 1737, Johnson had tried and failed three times to become a schoolteacher. The last and most substantial attempt at Edial, where he had invested his wife's money, failed a year later. Doubtless, this was the most disappointing of the three. Shortly afterward Johnson set out for London along with his student, David Garrick, so the familiar story goes. Ten years later he was approached by Dodsley to write on the subject of education for an audience much larger than he could ever have hoped to reach in a entire lifetime of teaching in a provincial school. In the persona of a master teacher he reached this larger audience of teachers and students combined not by his presence but by his absence, through the printed word.

Over the next fifteen years Johnson continued to reach the public through his writings until a royal pension in 1762 and his seventeen-year friendship with the prosperous and generous brewer Henry Thrale and Hester Thrale, his gifted wife, made it possible for him to write less and talk more. By the mid-to-late 1760s he had begun to become once again a teacher by his presence. But unlike

9

his earlier attempts, this one succeeded.[1] As a friend, a conversationalist, and a moral instructor, he addressed a circle of intimates and acquaintances who, unlike his students of the 1730s, were eager for his presence, wit, and learning. Perhaps, too, Johnson had changed over the years. He was, at last, no longer poor, frustrated, or young.[2]

There are at least two insights to be gained by telling the story of this portion of his life in this way, emphasizing his early attempts and failures at teaching, followed by the turn to writing, followed finally by a return to teaching through the pleasures of conversation. This account revitalizes the significance of Ian Watt's astute observation about Johnson and writing:

> Johnson is perhaps the supreme example of a great writer with very little sense of a specifically literary vocation. . . . If he thought of himself as an 'artist', it was in its eighteenth-century sense of a skilled craftsman; and his conception of how he should use his craft laid primary emphasis on his kinship with his fellow human beings.[3]

Writing was for him a second, indeed perhaps a third, choice of vocation. The practice of law, by inclination and desire, came first. Teaching, by circumstance, came second. And finally writing became his settled, if not precisely chosen, occupation. Considered in this way, it seems plausible to assume that Johnson would have thought of himself less as *a writer* and more as *one who wrote*. This is no small distinction. Its importance for thinking about this man as a creative agent as well as for examining our responses to his work will ramify throughout this study.

This way of telling the story of his early years also brings into more meaningful focus his profound lifelong fascination with how

1. Thomas M. Curley remarks that, although Johnson "failed in his school at Edial early in life, he spent the rest of his career successfully teaching the public old truths in new literary forms" (*Samuel Johnson and the Age of Travel*, 157–58). In a related vein John Wain comments that "everything, more or less, from *Rasselas* onward—reflects Johnson's knowledge that his immediate problems of survival are solved, that he can afford to devote the rest of his life to helping others to comb out the tangle of their conflicting impulses" (*Samuel Johnson*, 321).

2. Thomas Kaminski in *The Early Career of Samuel Johnson* has convincingly argued a revision of the traditional image of Johnson's poverty during the early London years (chapter 5, "Savage, Poverty, and Politics").

3. "Dr. Johnson," 18. Also see Paul Fussell on genre in *Samuel Johnson and the Life of Writing*, particularly chapter 2, "The Facts of Writing and the Johnsonian Senses of Literature."

people learn. For here are the beginnings of his special fascination with thinking biographically about education. Like many instances of such lifelong fascinations, this one is rooted in failure and dissatisfaction, which the subject eventually converts from liabilities into assets. These irritants, in the case of Johnson, served less as conventional seeds of Freudian compensation than as the direction and focus of an active and programmatic attention toward things and people throughout his life. His interest in how people learn was surely motivated as strongly by personal curiosity as by pedagogical and moral concerns. He knew the problem from the inside out because he too always had trouble giving full attention to his work and, by his own account, succeeded only once in his life. His having failed at teaching as a young man also argues the likelihood of a degree of personal involvement in an uncharacteristic remark in the *Life of Ascham* (1761). He comments that Ascham taught at a time when learning was "prosecuted with that eagerness and perseverance which in this age of indifference and dissipation it is not easy to conceive" and when "to teach or to learn was at once the business and the pleasure of the academical life."[4] Johnson rarely allowed himself to imagine better times in the past. He was not given to positing a prelapsarian age when things were as they should ideally be, because he considered such imagining perilously self-indulgent. Thus the remark about Ascham seems to offer evidence of disappointment and longing so strongly felt as to short-circuit his typically active skepticism.

His early failures as a teacher are perhaps also the seed of his doubt expressed in *Rambler* 87 (1751) about whether or not one can ever know another person well enough to teach him anything. While it is not uncharacteristic of Johnson to describe a seeming impossibility and then proceed to exhort us to attempt it nonetheless, his remarks about teaching and learning carry a uniquely para-

---

4. *The Life of Roger Ascham*, in *Early Biographical Writings of Dr. Johnson*, 498. In his study *Samuel Johnson: A Personality in Conflict*, George Irwin comments on Johnson's 1739 trip to the Grammar School at Appleby to apply for a position there: "For the fourth time Johnson had failed in his attempt to become a schoolmaster. Henceforth, until he was granted a royal pension in 1762, he earned his living with his pen; but so interwoven were his experiences of teaching with a sense of humiliation and failure that he could not for the rest of his life bear to be reminded of them" (83). While my study does not disagree with Irwin's remarks, it sets Johnson's personal disappointment within a larger and transforming context of how he used that experience objectively as well as continued to suffer from it personally.

doxical mix of pessimism and hope that are, even for him, uncommonly forceful and affecting.

His early disappointments, along with his choice of writing as a belated vocation, perhaps also combined to nurture in him a distinctive objectivity, born of a certain historically conventional detachment, toward writing. Among his contemporaries Johnson was, of course, not unique in this cultivated objectivity. It is a commonplace that eighteenth-century writers identified differently with their writing than did the writers of the following century, or at least projected a different appearance of identification. But if he was at one with his age on the matter of the writer's necessary (and even natural) objectivity, he was more solidly persuaded in this attitude than most and more committed to communicating it to his readers.

One is tempted to see in the episode of Dodsley's commission the operation of a kind of destiny directing Johnson to succeed where he had earlier failed, but now to succeed on a much larger scale than he had originally intended or could reasonably have hoped for.[5] This episode underscores an important aspect of his thinking that is rarely given sufficient emphasis, namely his imaginative interest in the importance of keeping one's eyes open for unexpected opportunities and, once seen, of using them well. Finally, it serves as a useful perspective from which to read both the Preface to *The Preceptor* and *The Vision of Theodore*, highlighting the qualities of mind that he brought to bear in examining how people teach and how they learn. It also suggests the corollary that his early experiences as a teacher, though unsuccessful if measured by conventional standards, may have triggered in him a distinctive sensitivity and provided him with more food for later thought than has heretofore been imagined.

None of the foregoing propositions can be proved, but together they serve the legitimate and valuable ends of helping to recover and account for the imaginative lucidity of his work for Dodsley. They also help account for why his thinking about education has proved compelling to readers in the twentieth century. And they may help explain why he thought so highly of his *Vision*. Against the backdrop of his early experiences as a teacher, which arguably

5. For details of the publication history of this preface see Hazen, *Samuel Johnson's Prefaces and Dedications*, 171–76. For an examination of the publication history and popularity of *The Vision* see Gwin J. Kolb's " 'The Vision of Theodore': Genre, Context, Early Reception," 107–24.

prepared him to explore his intuitions about how deeply lies the urge for education and how profoundly this urge orients us in the world, I hope to bring some heretofore unexamined aspects of Johnson into view. The commission from Dodsley may, in short, have touched a readiness in him to perceive, through the lens of his own failure, how central teaching and learning were in both his own and other people's lives.

Johnson understood education to be a fundamental act of living. Hence the reason for his being, at one and the same time, generally at home with the optimistic notions of his age about the possibilities and benefits of education, on the one hand, yet equally drawn to identifying the dangers and temptations that characteristically threaten successful education, on the other. For him, education was not merely one of the ways we improve ourselves; it was one of the basic and indispensable ways we communicate with and come to know others. In the two foregoing notions, Johnson's work bears strong affinities with such twentieth-century thinkers as Gregory Bateson and Michael Polanyi. These affinities in turn help to explain why the second half of our century has felt a particularly strong renewed kinship with Johnson. Polanyi comments, for instance, that the acquisition of knowledge is motivated by such deep forces of our being that repeated frustrations in problem-solving cause mental imbalances.[6] In his study of distortions of the learning process in schizophrenia, Bateson observes that "human beings have a commitment to the solutions which they discover, and it is this psychological commitment that makes it possible for them to be hurt in the way members of a schizophrenic family are hurt" by being "continually proven wrong whenever they have been wise."[7] Johnson, too, understood teaching and learning to be vital and instinctive habits, the lifelong urges of the healthy human soul.

It can be gathered from throughout his work that Johnson understood education to occur in two ways. The first was by slow disciplined movements toward truth, one step at a time; the second by unpredictable, though not unaccountable, surges and sudden insights that transform our being and reorient us in the world. The first notion coincides with the generally optimistic educational

6. Polanyi makes this argument in *Personal Knowledge: Towards a Post-Critical Philosophy.*
7. "The Group Dynamics of Schizophrenia," in *Steps to an Ecology of Mind: A Revolutionary Approach to Man's Understanding of Himself,* 242.

empiricism of the eighteenth century that he, to some degree, shared. But at the heart of Johnson's version of his century's empiricism is a skepticism of the kind that the twentieth century associates with Bertrand Russell's observation about how, given all the handicaps of obscurity and misunderstanding that threaten our attempts to learn and to communicate, the fact that we ever succeed in either activity is much more surprising than that we often fail. Precisely this kind of complex optimism motivates Johnson's other notion of the way we learn—the way not of empiricism but of rationalism. This rationalism is based on a belief not in the mind's power to gather, control, and communicate items of knowledge, but rather in *thinking itself* (not in the *thing being thought*) as a condition of expectancy that is the secular equivalent of religious faith.[8]

This manner of thinking that occurs in sudden unpredictable surges followed by radical reorientations is best illustrated by the familiar anecdote of the young Johnson at Oxford sitting down to read William Law's *Serious Call to a Devout and Holy Life* (1728). Expecting to find the book dull and laughable, he found himself instead overmatched by the author, who begins his essay with this assertion: "Devotion is neither private nor public prayer; but prayers, whether private or public, are particular parts or instances of devotion. Devotion signifies a life given, or devoted, to God."[9] Law does nothing less than reconceive devotion by defining prayer as a complete way of living, not a finite act. He considers devotion to be the whole of which life is a part. Gone are linear, incremental, and rational notions of prayer. Law's emphasis falls on the life lived, not the acts performed. Such a transformation calls upon the reader to reconceive devotion by making an instantaneous leap of

8. As Rodman D. Rhodes comments in, " 'Idler' No. 24 and Johnson's Epistemology," Johnson, in contrast to Locke, "considered the mind thinking to be of importance in itself." But he also believed, importing Locke's empiricism into Cartesian rationalism, that "the mind's dependence upon its environment is forever a 'state of life,' " and that "defining thought as the result of experience is not the equivalent of defining experience as the cause of thinking" (13, 14).

9. *A Serious Call to a Devout and Holy Life*, 1. On the subject of Samuel Johnson and William Law, see Katherine C. Balderston, "Dr. Johnson and William Law." She remarks in conclusion that "Law's dogmatic 'either-or' alternatives, his rigid perfectionism, and his limited and theoretical view of the real nature of men, were the earliest, and the strongest, external factors which forced Johnson's mind toward the need for realism, balance, and human insight in judging the complexities of the moral world" (394).

the imagination. No longer merely an activity or performance in the world, devotion is now recast as a decision made and hence a stance assumed in the knowledge of how religion bridges the gap between this world and the next. Johnson learned much about himself at an early age by discovering how susceptible he was to the imaginative power of Law's call.

BEING OF TWO MINDS: THE IMPORTANCE OF TRUST

The Preface to *The Preceptor* and *The Vision of Theodore* figure forth this view of Johnson's mind with its two distinct yet intertwined attitudes on the subject of how we learn. Such is my point of view toward this early pair of writings which, in turn, will serve as the sketch of his mind to introduce the succeeding chapters. The Preface is a political essay in the characteristically Johnsonian sense of what constitutes politics, namely the hierarchical distribution of power. He recognized that education, like any activity involving a commodity (in this case knowledge), which some people have and some do not, creates a hierarchy of superiors and inferiors. Hierarchies inevitably threaten trust and make confidence problematic because implicit in these structures are temptations to the abuse of power.

In *Sermon* 8 he elaborates this insight with sympathy and precision:

> There is no employment in which men are more easily betrayed to indecency and impatience, than in that of teaching; in which they necessarily converse with those, who are their inferiours, in the relation by which they are connected, and whom it may be sometimes proper to treat with that dignity which too often swells into arrogance; and to restrain with such authority as not every man has learned to separate from tyranny. (YJ 14:92)

The passage acutely analyzes the temptations to tyranny and other abuses of power endemic to teaching. Recognizing these dangers that chronically endanger education, his Preface to *The Preceptor* encourages a pragmatic confidence in the natural movements of the student's mind. Because application and will naturally follow interest and confidence, teachers must beware of undermining their students' trust in the reliability of these movements of mind.

Johnson's age provided a context for such thoughts as these and also for a belief in the importance of accurately observing how the mind actually does work before designing a plan to educate it. But his thoughts on education are also distinctively his own. He emphasizes how the student's interest should take precedence over the teacher's plans and theories and how teachers must be perpetually alert to temptations to tyrannize over their students. Early in the Preface he comments on the difficulty of keeping students' attention focused on their work:

> Every Man, who has been engaged in Teaching, knows with how much Difficulty youthful Minds are confined to close Application, and how readily they deviate to any thing, rather than attend to that which is imposed as a Task. That this Disposition, when it becomes inconsistent with the Forms of Education, is to be checked, will readily be granted; but since, though it may be in some Degree obviated, it cannot wholly be suppressed, it is surely rational to turn it to Advantage, by taking Care that the Mind shall never want Objects on which its Faculties may be usefully employed. (PD 176)

As often characterizes his advice, this passage begins with a general observation, namely that young minds wander from imposed tasks. He advises that, on balance, such wandering should be checked. But his recommendation expands rather than limits the possibilities for exploring the subject. We readily grant the theoretical correctness of such advice, yet it remains to be considered how such a theory can be decently and efficiently applied to people's actual behavior. Johnson is habitually intrigued by the challenge of application both on account of its difficulty as a problem to solve and for its practical importance as a recognition of the real stakes of learning.

He begins by introducing three key notions in the phrase, "though it may be in some Degree *obviated*, it cannot wholly be *suppressed*, it is surely rational to *turn it to Advantage*" (emphasis mine). These notions will serve as the main points of his agenda for turning educational liabilities into assets. He admits the disappointing discrepancy between what we "will readily grant" as theoretically the teacher's ideal course of action, on the one hand, and what we are forced to admit rationally when we examine how people actually behave, on the other.

Johnson's critical mapping of this common situation has already moved some distance toward a solution—from the phenomenon of the student's wandering mind to the theoretical correctness of suppressing inattention, to the reasonable aim of obviating this problem, and finally to the possibility of transforming a liability into an asset. But such a transformation must first occur in the teacher's imagination before it can become educational practice. Teachers must see the situation anew before their attitude and hence their behavior can be transformed. Behavior formerly measured by the ideal of toeing certain preconceived marks (the application of norms of correct and incorrect behavior) is now provisionally revised to admit the possibility that any movement of the student's mind may be educationally advantageous. If a teacher values the student's single-mindedness over and above all other qualities, then the student's wandering attention will necessarily be perceived as an instance of misbehavior and hence as a serious obstacle to successful learning. But if educational practice is recast to admit the desirability of placing several objects before the mind, then the student's wandering attention is seen in a different light. Such revisions were of perennial interest to Johnson both for their practical use and as evidence of hope serving to structure the operations of the imagination.

So far he has discussed the phenomena of education as they take form in the student's behavior and the teacher's practice. He now considers the possible origins of the student's "restless Desire of Novelty":

> It is not impossible, that this restless Desire of Novelty, which gives so much Trouble to the Teacher, may be often the Struggle of the Understanding starting from that, to which it is not by Nature adapted, and travelling in Search of something on which it may fix with greater Satisfaction. For without supposing each Man, particularly marked out by his Genius for particular Performances, it may be easily conceived, that when a numerous Class of Boys is confined indiscriminately to the same Forms of Composition, the Repetition of the same Words, or the Explication of the same Sentiments, the Employment, must either by Nature or Accident be differently received by them. (PD 176–77)

This substantive portrait of the young mind's fears and yearnings, of how it withdraws fearfully from what it does not know and is drawn reassuringly toward what it already knows, suggests how much Johnson had learned from his early attempts at teaching.

While avoiding the error of asserting innate and particular genius, he does in this description allow for differences of nature or accident in the way students learn:

> Every Mind in its Progress through the different Stages of scholastic Learning, must be often in some of these Circumstances, must either flag with the Labour, or grow wanton with the Facility of the Work assigned; and in either State it naturally turns aside from the Track before it. Weariness looks out for Relief, and Leisure for Employment, and surely it is rational to indulge the Wanderings of both. (PD 177)

A paradox, but one for which the Preface has by now prepared the reader, the argument for indulging the wanderings of weariness and leisure assents to human limitations and identifies that assent as evidence of reason. This argument also lays the groundwork for Johnson's emphasis on the importance of giving individual attention to students, since "it is observable, that though very few read well, yet every Man errs in a different Way" (PD 180). As students err in different ways, so they also learn in different ways. Errors, like accuracy, taken cumulatively, are revealing biographical records. A responsible educational theory and practice must take into account students' distinctive styles of both mastering and failing to master. Thus the history of one's education, its successes and failures, is a record of identity crucial, in turn, to learning.

Yet Johnson also reckons with the limits of education thus empirically conceived:

> It is not to be doubted but that Logicians may be sometimes overborn by their Passions, or blinded by their Prejudices . . . but because he does not regard it; yet it is not more the Fault of his Art that it does not direct him when his Attention is withdrawn from it, than it is the Defect of his Sight that he misses his Way when he shuts his Eyes. (PD 185)

Learning an art or discipline neither guarantees nor explains the reason for its use. No discipline teaches itself. Motive and habit must be learned separately from application and skill, although neither can application and skill succeed alone. He always takes these facts into account. In *The Vision of Theodore* he maps their ethical territory.

Habit for Johnson mediates between the empirical and rational models of mind and knowledge. The empirical model, conceiving of education as an activity that organizes parts into a coherent whole, is optimistic in its strategies yet severely limited in its conception. This model does not carry within itself the motive for its use, nor acknowledge that education is, even in its seemingly most objective and impersonal guises, a personal and intersubjective experience. Learning chiefly occurs between people, an issue that Chapter 4 of this study will more fully elaborate. Hence the origin of education's complexity and its susceptibility to the corruptions of power that always threaten to erode the mutual trust between teacher and student. Theirs is a relationship that, by its very structure, is politically imbalanced. From this structural imbalance follow psychological and epistemological implications.

Johnson's pessimism is, however, equally constitutive of hope. For it defines the location of a principle that, lying outside education, can thereby apply needed leverage to it. This principle serves the important function of organizing learning, not from parts to whole but from whole to parts, by providing a pattern to shape the whole. Habit, as *The Vision of Theodore* dramatizes, serves for good, though sometimes for ill, just such a function.

BEING OF TWO MINDS: THE NECESSITY OF MISTRUST IN *THE VISION OF THEODORE*

Among our contemporaries, James L. Clifford was the first to understand Johnson's preference for *The Vision*, finding that preference not only comprehensible but "also helpful in the way it offers contemporary readers the encouragement and angle we seem to need in order to approach one of Johnson's less available and inviting works." Clifford's comment that "the tale is a perfect statement of his moral creed" gave early expression to what has become the majority opinion. He grants that modern readers may find the tale "too sententious," too allegorical. Yet, he continues, "the abstract figures do seem to live, and there is a fascination about the troop of Habits, who lie in wait to ensnare travelers on the mountain of Existence, swelling or diminishing as they are welcomed or repelled." Clifford concludes by observing that this work may offer a clue to one of Johnson's principal fears, his fear of sloth, projected in the description of the travelers lost the maze of Indolence.[10] John Wain, finding *The Vision* a "sombre and beautiful fable," is in the minority in mentioning no difficulties for modern readers.[11] Like Clifford, Richard B. Schwartz argues that this tale "is particularly relevant as an index to Johnson's own intellectual allegiances" and deserves far more attention than it has been given.[12] This is still generally the case, though Lawrence Lipking has contributed substantially to the reputation and comprehension of this allegory as central to Johnson's ways of thinking. He remarks on how we generally agree that there is always something to be learned about a great writer "by considering the work that he himself thought his

10. *Young Sam Johnson*, 306–7.
11. *Samuel Johnson*, 149.
12. "Johnson's 'Vision of Theodore,' " 31. Carey McIntosh in *The Choice of Life: Samuel Johnson and the World of Fiction* identifies "a certain menacing quality in Johnson's allegories" (113).

best." Lipking proposes that "at his most heroic, Johnson demands—and trains—an audience of heroes."[13]

To my knowledge, only Walter Jackson Bate finds Johnson's preference for the piece both incomprehensible and more than a little embarrassing. His remarks bear thinking about, less to assess their plausibility, though plausibility is demanded of genetic criticism, than to consider their grounds, which bear upon my central premise about biographical thinking—its motives, dangers, and uses. Bate sees Johnson's preference for this work as "so absurd that we can forgivably assume one of two things. On some occasion when Percy was praising Johnson's allegories, which he genuinely admired, Johnson could have pulled his leg by making a remark of this sort. Or Johnson may have been referring only to Oriental tales and allegories, and stating that he thought this the best of the lot (the remark was made before he wrote *Rasselas*)." Bate also comments, in marked contrast to Clifford: "It is amusing to see him, even at this busy time, as apprehensive as ever at the capacity of Indolence to hand one over to Melancholy and Despair."[14]

These remarks are surprising on several counts. Bate's perceiving a comic incongruity between Johnson's busy career at the time of writing *The Vision* and his apprehensiveness about indolence seems not to have taken into account the insight otherwise so consistently evident in his biography, namely that one's feelings, in this case one's fears, may continue despite substantial evidence against them. Emotions, especially those associated with guilt, live a powerful life of their own. Furthermore, the comment assumes at one and the same time both too little and too much involvement between a writer's work and his life. Why does Bate assume on the one hand that the portrait of Indolence dramatizes the author's uneasiness, while on the other that Johnson's busy engagement in work would assuage his anxieties about indolence? And why would the critic assume the duty of protecting Johnson (a presumption, if not a condescension) by imagining two possible, complicated intentions behind his praise of *The Vision*, which are, if not farfetched, at least not so near at hand as the assumption that he meant what he said? To apply to the interpretation of recorded conversation Johnson's own editorial principal about taking words

13. "Learning to Read Johnson: *The Vision of Theodore* and *The Vanity of Human Wishes*," 517, 526.
14. *Samuel Johnson*, 253n, 253.

in texts at face value, rather than straining for distant or obscure meaning, cues us to interpret Johnson's praise in the simplest way possible when there is no more compelling reason to read it otherwise.

Johnson's allegory of education tells the story of the Hermit of Teneriffe who one day experiences a strong desire to leave the spot he has occupied for forty-eight years of exile. He begins to climb, grows tired, and falls asleep, only to find himself awakened by a figure who guides him on a visionary tour of the Mountain of Existence. From the base the travelers are shepherded by Innocence, who soon gives them over into Education's care. Hereafter they choose between the guides Reason and Religion. All the while, they are accompanied by a band of habits. This varied, delusory, and fascinating group are pygmies. At any moment and without warning, whenever the travelers grow careless, these figures may suddenly enlarge into dangerous adversaries.

In the many details Johnson invents to dramatize the psychosomatic force of habits and to make this word an emotionally as well as a morally resonant notion, he identifies a concept that William James, a century and a half later, was to name the "secret of will." James observes that the idea of being a drunkard is precisely what

> will not stay before the poor soul's attention. But if he once gets able to pick out that way of conceiving, from all the other possible ways of conceiving the various opportunities which occur, if through thick and thin he holds to it that this is being a drunkard and is nothing else, he is not likely to remain one long. The effort by which he succeeds in keeping the right *name* unwaveringly present to his mind proves to be his saving moral act.[15]

James, like Johnson, dramatizes habits in a way calculated to help readers truly become acquainted with these dangers. Johnson's portrait likewise emphasizes the independent reality of habits, their powerful capacity to organize and thereby tyrannize behavior. His portrait is lengthy, the details accumulating with insight and power:

> It was observable, that their stature was never at a stand, but continually growing or decreasing, yet not always in the same proportions; nor could I forbear to express my admiration, when I saw in how much less time they generally gained than lost bulk. . . . It was the peculiar artifice of Habit not to suffer her power to be felt at first. Those whom

15. *The Principles of Psychology,* 2:565.

> she led, she had the address of appearing only to attend, but was continually doubling her chains upon her companions; which were so slender in themselves, and so silently fastened, that while the attention was engaged by other objects, they were not easily perceived. Each link grew tighter as it had been longer worn, and when, by continual additions they became so heavy as to be felt, they were very frequently too strong to be broken. . . . The manner in which those who were weary of their tyranny endeavoured to escape from them, appeared by the event to be generally wrong; they tried to loose their chains one by one, and to retreat by the same degrees as they advanced; but before the deliverance was completed, Habit always threw new chains upon her fugitive: nor did any escape her but those who by an effort sudden and violent, burst their shackles at once, and left her at a distance; and even of these many rushing too precipitately forward, and hindered by their terrors from stopping where they were safe, were fatigued with their own vehemence, and resigned themselves again to that power from whom an escape must be so dearly bought, and whose tyranny was little felt, except when it was resisted. (YJ 16:201, 202, 207)

This dramatization of habits is bold in outline and nuanced in detail. The gathering evidence directs the reader to draw only one possible conclusion, namely that the tyranny of habits must be immediately and completely overturned. Delay becomes inconceivable. The appropriate cure is thus asymmetrically related to the disease. Yet this cure, Johnson notes, carries its own danger. Overturning dangerous habits fatigues the travelers, often making them vulnerable to their adversaries once again. In victory are the seeds of subsequent defeat. Finally he notes the curious phenomenology of habits, principally defined by two characteristics: They exist and operate unfelt, and they can be perceived only when they are being resisted.

By contrast with his depiction of the chronic dangers of habits, Johnson creates only one scene to dramatize their virtuous operations. Those few travelers who actually succeed in remaining on the path of religion find that, while the habits threaten to sabotage their journey, they may also help to keep them on the straight and narrow path:

> Every other power was easily resisted, nor did they find any difficulty when they inadvertently quitted her [Religion], to find her again by the direction of Conscience, unless they had given time to Habit to draw her chain behind them, and bar up the way by which they had wandered. . . . But if by a timely call upon Religion, the force of Habit was eluded, her attacks grew fainter, and at last her correspondence with the enemy was entirely destroyed. She then began to employ those restless faculties in compliance with the power which she could not

overcome; and as she grew again in stature and in strength, cleared away the asperities of the road to Happiness. (YJ 16:206, 208)

This allegory of habits, like James's later version, proposes how crucial to the cure is finding the appropriate name for an addiction. Accurate naming empowers the addict to keep the addictive condition in the forefront of consciousness. Until this is accomplished, the addiction will continue. For Johnson, as for James, such consciousness is the primary and distinguishing act of the moral intelligence.

The Vision of Theodore dramatizes the important insight that the few truths we really need are neither difficult, though they may be demanding, nor distant, though they may not be accessible through conventional linear routes that assemble a whole from its constitutive parts. Because habits cannot be perceived sequentially, they cannot be revised one after another. Like devotion, they are not merely the result or accumulation of a series of acts, but rather the performance of an attitude toward world, self, and whatever may lie beyond that is practical equipment for living, significant yet also elementary enough for the young readers of Dodsley's anthology to master.

One final aspect of Johnson's phenomenology of habits must be considered, namely his commitment to a pair of equally valued positions that may at first glance seem mutually contradictory. The first is his sense of the importance of trustworthiness in human relations; the second, his sense of the importance of a perpetual distrust of our own hearts. Regarding the first, he understood that a fundamental degree of mutual trust is necessary in order for us to function in this life. The basic operations of the social system depend on the generally reliable exchange of information, whatever form that information may take, whether facts, opinions, or feelings. We must be able generally to rely on people telling us the truth. If such information is not on balance true, the whole system collapses. Truth is not an abstract moral value or a disembodied responsibility. It is a necessity for survival. Lying, by contrast, attacks the very circuit of communication that defines and structures society. Here, from *Sermon* 18, is Johnson's description of fraud as a profoundly violent and antisocial act precisely because it abuses confidence:

But deceit cannot be practised, unless by some previous treaty, and gradual advance, by which distrust is dissipated, and an opinion of candour and integrity excited. *Fraud*, therefore, necessarily disguises life with solicitude and suspicion. He that has been deceived, knows not afterwards whom he can trust, but grows timorous, reserved, afraid alike of enemies and friends; and loses, at least, part of that benevolence which is necessary to an amiable and virtuous character. . . . It has been always observed by the wise, that it is every man's real interest to be honest; and he who practises *fraud*, to the injury of others, shews, at the same time, how *fraud* may be practised against himself. (YJ 14:198–99, 200)

Even if aimed at only one person, the lie always damages society as a whole by corrupting the system of communicative confidence upon which everyone relies.[16] Hence the origin of Johnson's concern, apparent in his early Preface to *The Preceptor* and sustained throughout his career, with the issue of honesty in teaching. He repeatedly warns teachers against abusing their power either by the inadvertent violence of impatience or by the calculated sin of easy tyranny over those who, by virtue of their circumstances alone, are less powerful than themselves. Trust is the very condition and ground of education. In turn, education is the archetype of all human exchanges because it depends on shared confidence. Holding such beliefs, it is not surprising that he emphasizes the importance of teachers valuing their students' trust as an absolute necessity for successful teaching.

While he advises teachers to value and protect this intersubjective trust, so he advises students to be skeptical toward themselves. This advice is the chief lesson of *The Vision*, which is reciprocally related to Johnson's thinking about religion. As he proposes confidence to be the great force driving successful teaching, so he observes in *Sermon* 3 that religion traditionally proposes fear as its principle: "[Religion] implicitly condemns all self-confidence, all presumptuous security; and enjoins a constant state of vigilance and caution, a perpetual distrust of our own hearts, a full conviction of our natural weakness, and an earnest solicitude for divine assistance" (YJ 14:30). Theodore, who at the outset is a conventionally self-doubting hermit, learns during the course of his journey a yet more severe lesson about the necessity of an even more powerful self-doubt. As he studies the Mountain of Existence with his spiritual guide, a figure gentle and trustworthy, he learns and practices the techniques for a yet sterner course of self-scrutiny.

16. Sissela Bok's *Lying: Moral Choice in Public and Private Life* examines these and other aspects of lying.

AN UNSTABLE BALANCE

If mental health and the ability to function as relative social beings depend on intersubjective trust, spiritual health depends on our perpetual mistrust of ourselves. Throughout his career Johnson sharpened his sensitivity to the benefits and responsibilities of cultivating this complex perspective on education, which this chapter has examined and will now summarize in closing.

The Preface sketches a portrait of education as a group endeavor in which the participants relate to one another hierarchically. Hierarchy is inevitable whenever resources and skills are unequally divided. Thus education is, by its nature, risky business. Teachers are chronically susceptible to temptations to misuse their superiority. Students are liable to fears and dangers resulting from their inferiority. These problems, endemic to education, must be consciously considered. Since Johnson believed that education depends on successful and honest group endeavor, it follows that tyranny and betrayal, because they undermine the process at its most basic level, would have gravely disturbed him. Since teaching and learning were for him a figure for human interdependence, it also follows that, from his point of view, their success or failure implicates us all, not just those who are officially denominated students and teachers.

The possibilities for succeeding or failing in education turn on the single, unstable fact that other people's behavior can neither be predicted with certainty nor controlled with precision. Here *The Vision* and the Preface interconnect and form a kind of philosophical Möbius strip, each part of which begins where the other ends, each part responding to the questions that the other, by virtue of its particular perspective and presuppositions, cannot answer. Where, if not in others, may we hope to find the predictability and control we long for? The familiar Johnsonian answer is in ourselves.

While the rational answer is easy to come by, the practical solution is usually much more difficult. Johnson makes a clear and functional distinction between unmemorable answers that envision the terms of a solution rhetorically and memorable answers that envision a whole life context as the scene of their accomplishment. He understood very well the difficulties—those much-practiced arts of self-delusion and the high stakes involved in continuing to believe that we are personally exempt from the general fate. But he also perceived the simplicity of self-control, understood to be not the cause of certain effects but rather an orientation toward and within life that empowers certain kinds of behavior. This kind of perception motivated his admiration for Law's definition of devotion, not as something one does, but as a way of doing all things. Such thinking also shapes Johnson's high valuing of auto-biography on account of its empowering truthfulness, less allied to subject matter than to method. Few of us, he once observed, tell lies only to ourselves. He did not believe honesty to be easy. But he did believe that the best approach to achieving honesty involves a method deliberately and methodologically naive. Why would any-one lie when lying will almost certainly never succeed in the end?

This insight identifies a position from which can be seen with perfect clarity that we have no real reason to lie to ourselves. John-son is interested in the usefulness of a point of view from which such a vision not only is possible but indeed is the only possible vision.[17] It becomes the only possible vision not because tempta-tion disappears or because human ingenuity for self-delusion sud-denly evaporates, but rather because, like Law's definition of devo-tion and like the viewpoint of those teachers who no longer indulge in easy tyranny over their students, there intervenes another view-point from which the lie becomes unthinkable. Thus the truth becomes both perfectly clear and unquestionably compelling. It becomes a habit no longer requiring conscious recollection because it is now the ground of both thought and action. Considered to-gether, the Preface to *The Preceptor* and *The Vision of Theodore* embody Johnson's version of the relation between thinking and believing formulated for us by Gregory Bateson: " 'The truth can-not be said so as to be understood, and not be believed,' but, con-versely, it cannot be believed *until* it is said so as to be understood."[18]

---

17. Paul K. Alkon identifies the interaction of description and exhortation in *Samuel Johnson and Moral Discipline* when he observes, for instance, that "a striking feature of Johnson's prose is the relative infrequency of imperative sentences: the great moralist seldom commands" (ix).

18. "Minimal Requirements for a Theory of Schizophrenia," in *Steps to an Ecology of Mind*, 250.

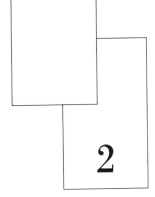

2 ACQUAINTANCE AND KNOWLEDGE

The Prefaces to the *Dictionary* and *The Plays of William Shakespeare*

AT HOME WITH BEGINNINGS AND ENDINGS

By temperament and training Johnson's mind was always at home with beginnings and endings. First things and last were literally and figuratively his strength. Chapter 1 examined this temperament as expressed in his work for Dodsley's *Preceptor.* Teaching the virtues of hard work, patience, and trust, his preface is grounded in an optimistic educational psychology embodying a cheerful sense of beginning. By contrast, *The Vision of Theodore* is guided by the sense of ending, the precedence of last things in our present lives, the need for systematic self-doubt and, from time to time, for radical reorientations that cannot be achieved by merely logical or linear thinking.

Johnson's mind was also one that educated itself "by fits and starts, by violent irruptions."[1] His rhythms of learning were alternately lethargic and ferocious. Inspired perhaps in part by his own rhythms of thought, in part by his sense of the brevity of life, implying the responsibility to use our time well, he once commented: "I fancy mankind may come, in time, to write all aphoristically, except in narrative; grow weary of preparation, and connection, and illustration, and all those arts by which a big book is made."[2] The big book, he recognized, has many drawbacks from both the writer's and reader's points of view.

He had reason from his own experience to trust the impulses of sudden interest to direct his studies. This was how he learned most of what he knew. His mind was uneasy with lengthy argumenta-

1. James Boswell, *Boswell's Life of Johnson*, 1:97.
2. Ibid., 5:39.

tion, perhaps even depressed by it.[3] He rarely read a book all the way through for several reasons. He knew how limited is our time for learning and for doing; he believed that all truly necessary knowledge is self-evident and near at hand; he conceived of learning as a personal, perhaps even an eccentric activity; and he felt that no learning became genuinely one's own until it had been made in some fundamental sense a personal possession. He perceived this transformation to occur at both ends of the learning process. For the same reason that learning by rote is not true learning so, too, reading a book is useless if readers do not first consider what they already know on the subject and imagine how they would have written about it. A sense of self is crucial to learning.

This portrait of the man thinking implies yet another of his characteristic insights into the nature of learning, namely the importance of acquaintance. He considered education not to be an activity involving definition and explanation as its chief modes of understanding, but rather to be one involving the exchanges of acquaintance, in the sense we mean when we talk about coming to know another person. This kind of knowing involves comprehension through time based on the recognition of patterns of behavior, thought, and feeling. He conceived of the preface, as genre, to embody this notion of learning by acquaintance. His introduction to Baretti's *Guide Through the Royal Academy* (1781) illustrates this view of what the preface should do:

> To those, whom either vagrant curiosity, or desire of instruction, brings into the Apartments of the Royal Academy, not to know the design, the history, and the names of the various Models that stand before them, is a great abatement of pleasure, and hindrance of improvement. He who enters, not knowing what to expect, gazes a while about him, a stranger among strangers, and goes out, not knowing what he has seen. (PD 12)

To visit the Royal Academy without preparation is purposeless. Having entered unprepared, one would surely leave unacquainted, not knowing what one has seen. Without prior acquaintance, the visitor looks without seeing. Learning involves knowing in advance by establishing a history of expectation. New understanding must carry the force of genuine repetition and of prior acquaintance in order to become truly our own.

3. Donald Greene comments that Johnson seems to be "constitutionally incapable of an extended effort of logical organization" (" 'Logical Structure' in Eighteenth-Century Poetry," 331).

Johnson's insight into the importance of genuine repetition for education has its predecessors, including most notably the Platonic notion of education as recollection. But his imaginative attention to this commonplace and his emphasis on the drama of acquaintance with its biographical associations as a model of learning are very much his own. It is just such a model of successful learning that informs his two major prefaces, to the *Dictionary* (1755) and to his edition of *The Plays of William Shakespeare* (1765).

Prefaces face in two directions at once. Because they are usually written after the main body of the work is completed, they are for the author a backward glance; for the reader they are a preview. In the historical doubleness of the preface, a fact of its history embodied in its structure, lies the origin of its powers of acquaintance and the source of the fascination it held for Johnson. He was drawn to looking forward and back. He believed that he did both well, once remarking to Sir Joshua Reynolds:

> There are two things which I am confident I can do very well: one is an introduction to any literary work, stating what it is to contain, and how it should be executed in the most perfect manner; the other is a conclusion, shewing from various causes why the execution has not been equal to what the authour promised to himself and to the publick.[4]

Confident in his ability to write introductions and conclusions, he was equally certain that authors will always disappoint both themselves and their readers. He pokes fun at the writers of conclusions, including himself, who justify their own work by criticizing the writing they assess. At the same time, however, he recognizes this criticism to be an outcropping of the universal condition of disappointment that prevails no less in assessing one's own achievements than in measuring other people's. Thus writers of conclusions are doubly doomed. They are doomed by their occupation to note the shortcomings of others and doomed by the force of accumulated evidence to expect that they will also disappoint themselves. Theirs is an unhappy consciousness.

In the way the two major prefaces simultaneously introduce the reader to the work and conclude the author's undertaking, each thereby folding back upon itself, they identify the same general truth about the writer's responsibility to acknowledge the historical reality of reader and writer. Specifically, each identifies how the reader's and writer's positions in time, relative to one another

4. Boswell, *Life*, 1:292.

and to their respective subject matter, are crucial to their acquaintance. Successful acquaintance is especially important for works as lengthy and time-consuming as a dictionary of the language and an edition of Shakespeare. By their very nature and by the degree of intense and lengthy work necessary to complete them, they tempt their authors into solipsism. The dictionary maker may become "lost in lexicography," while the editor may come to think of himself as more important than his author. To both dangers Johnson is acutely sensitive.

Critics have commented on Johnson's role-playing, hyperbole, self-irony, and his "big bow wows" in the prefaces to the *Dictionary* and to *Shakespeare*. They have also commented on how comparing the 1755 Preface and the 1746 *Plan* identifies a Johnson who, as Howard Weinbrot writes, grew and changed from "the brash young man flexing his muscles, convinced of his own omnipotence, but incapable of so convincing us" to "the mature and weary man, with a huge effort behind him, and a realization of the failings of the human situation within him."[5] But there is more to be seen in this relationship between the objective and self-reflexive aspects of Johnson's role-playing, particularly as these combine to educate the reader by acquaintance. This chapter will examine that relationship.

Lionel T. Basney has observed that Johnson used role-playing in his public and private lives as a way of inquiring into moral and epistemological problems.[6] This role-playing is fundamentally projective and biographical. He imagines himself as others, or imagines otherness in himself, and thus inquires with special energy and acuteness. These insights combine in interesting ways with several other aspects of his career as a writer of prefaces. It is well known that he wrote prefaces on an extraordinary range of subjects implying the range of his general knowledge. It is equally well known that he often wrote them for friends and sometimes for people, such as Milton's niece, to whom he felt a sense of civic obligation.[7] He sometimes studied a subject for the sole purpose of writing a preface. And he sometimes wrote prefaces to books that he undertook to introduce without having read, confident that he

---

5. "Samuel Johnson's *Plan* and Preface to the *Dictionary*, 94.
6. " 'Ah ha!—Sam Johnson!—I see thee!': Johnson's Ironic Roles."
7. See Robert Folkenflik's essay, "That Man's Scope," on the intellectual range of Johnson's prefaces.

could imagine what any reader would need to know before beginning them.

Taken together, these details compose a picture of the Johnson who wrote prefaces. This activity called into play his ranging and various knowledge and invoked his ability to master quickly adequate working knowledge of a subject. It gave him the opportunity to apply his belief in the importance of acquaintance as a preparation for explanation, as well as to perform his generosity in writing. Thus from his preface writing, a metonymic biography of the man might be written, one that, given his own prediction that one day readers will tire of the arts by which the big book is made, might even have held particular interest for Johnson himself.

The subject of the present chapter can also be conceived in a slightly different way by noting how in both the major prefaces he treats the subject matter as important not only for its own sake but also for the way it provides an occasion to consider how we know what we know. He recognized that the subject matter of each preface (the English language in one, Shakespeare's drama in the other), takes no small part of its significance from the way it opens out onto larger and ever-interesting questions about knowledge, the getting of knowledge, and about the indispensability of confidence to the enterprise of knowing. He understood precisely how, in order to approach a formidable undertaking, like a dictionary of the language or an edition of plays, readers must feel sufficiently confident to make the first approach.[8] Both of his major prefaces substantially and honestly encourage readers that they are already equipped to use these books.

ACQUAINTING THE READER WITH THE *DICTIONARY*

Johnson characteristically begins a preface and commences the drama of acquaintance by depicting some aspect of the psychology of the task that lies behind the writing and ahead of the reading. In the Preface to the *Dictionary* he characterizes the psychology of all those "who toil at the lower employments of life" and who are thus fated "to be rather driven by the fear of evil, than attracted by the prospect of good." To acquaint us with a typically invisible workingman, he invokes the force of melodrama to bring that figure into view and to make his fate, for a moment, interesting to us. In his

---

8. James L. Clifford discusses Johnson's talent for inspiring confidence in his readers in *Dictionary Johnson: Samuel Johnson's Middle Years*, 181.

depiction of the dictionary maker he assumes a tone in equal parts self-aggrandizing and self-deprecating. This combination makes visible what was formerly unseen. It is a first step toward learning. Identifying the lexicographer's conventional invisibility ("to be exposed to censure, without hope of praise; to be disgraced by miscarriage, or punished for neglect, where success would have been without applause, and diligence without reward"), Johnson suggests that this writer, like his subject, language, is difficult to see. He will suggest, as the Preface unfolds, that these two invisibilities are no mere coincidence and that their interrelation has important implications for the study of language.

If it is melodramatic to say, as he does, that the lexicographer alone among authors "can only hope to escape reproach," this statement, nevertheless, serves a useful purpose. It acquaints the reader with the distinctive kind of intelligence required to make and to use a dictionary. Some writing promises, as the alternative to failure, glory; not so the making of a dictionary. This characteristic serves as prologue to the information that follows about the lexicographer's distinctive kind of work—work that bears the burden of serious responsibilities but which by its very nature and in proportion to meeting its responsibilities cannot soar. This information, in turn, offers a kind of insider's knowledge, educating readers to use the dictionary from the inside out and thus more confidently.

Having described the grand but thankless labors of the dictionary maker, he begins the next paragraph comically: "I have, notwithstanding this discouragement, attempted a dictionary of the *English* language." The preceding two paragraphs with their catalog of the heroic labors and the fated liabilities of such work are condensed and displaced by three words: "notwithstanding this discouragement." This phrase functions in relation to the preceding paragraph in several different, though fundamentally related ways. Compressing the catalog of mighty endeavors and miseries into the single general term *discouragement*, Johnson dignifies and distances himself from the calculated melodrama of the opening paragraphs. He thus moves us into a different frame of reference, relocating us outside the frame where the author's fate is determined by his readers and into a space where his success is measured relative only to himself. He has, after all, now completed the dictionary. This fact is certain; it is not contingent on other people's opinions. And this certainty casts a different light on the earlier hyperbole. Because it signifies a psychological victory over the discouragement that characteristically plagues major efforts, completing a project of such magnitude is no small success.

Having brought into view two previously invisible dramas, he now describes a third drama in order to explain why he made a dictionary: "while it [the English language] was employed in the cultivation of every species of literature, has itself been hitherto neglected." If there is educational melodrama in the lexicographer's fate, there is a similar usefulness in this history of the neglect of our language. By calling into question our general complacency regarding language, he brings it newly into view, evoking our curiosity to consider what language is and how we use it. Such revision not only sheds new light on the particular subject in question by making it newly visible but also more generally and perhaps more importantly instructs the reader in imagining difference and in thinking biographically about difference. These issues of perception are among the chief subjects of the Preface. The study of language is, as Johnson knew, a study of the ways we differ from our contemporaries and even from ourselves over time. It is also a study of the ways we, as creatures in and of history, differ from those who have preceded and those who will follow us. The differences in what we see and the seeing of differences are fundamental aspects of who we are.

His comments on the paradoxical invisibility of language and our subsequent failure to study one of the mediums of life leads to another observation about how language can be studied only with language. It is both the medium being studied and the instrument of study.[9] From the initial depiction of the invisible dictionary maker Johnson has drawn our attention, in several stages, to the paradoxical nature of the task of definition. The transparency of language is an ordinary fact of experience that seems odd only when we try to think about it consciously. As in walking one does not think about every step, so in speaking one does not concentrate on the individual words—a fact made visible by the dictionary. By bringing

9. See Cyril H. Knoblauch's comment in the essay "Coherence Betrayed: Samuel Johnson and the 'Prose of the World'" that the "Dictionary as a text is especially complicated because language serves there as both the instrument and the object of critical evaluation. It is an autobiography of language, symbolic action mirroring its own motions" (241). Knoblauch also comments on the way the Dictionary "excites its reader to share and interact with a personal struggle toward meaning" (247–48).

into the foreground what usually constitutes the background and thus making visible what is generally unseen, a dictionary does more than define words. By acquainting readers consciously with their habits of perception, a dictionary, so Johnson proposes, makes available the pleasures of recognition and of learning what we already in some sense know but have yet to consider consciously. Such awareness is central to successful learning.

Having made language visible as an object of investigation, he now recalls mock-heroically the first stage of his work:

> When I took the first survey of my undertaking, I found our speech copious without order, and energetick without rules: wherever I turned my view, there was perplexity to be disentangled, and confusion to be regulated; choice was to be made out of boundless variety, without any established principle of selection; adulterations were to be detected, without a settled test of purity; and modes of expression to be rejected or received, without the suffrages of any writers of classical reputation or acknowledged authority.

As he uses personae to inquire into moral and epistemological problems, so too he uses them to dramatize the psychology of effort and the dream of scholarly heroism. To undertake a major project presupposes substantial motivation. Motivation, in turn, is largely an invention of the appropriate terms of interest in and hope for the project—terms that are always in large part personal and thus cumulatively describe a life. Hyperbole, as Johnson dramatizes it to illustrate his point, is always a danger. But its all too frequent alternative is boredom, a far more threatening condition, which he would examine at length in *Rasselas* four years later. As Chapter 4 will examine, whatever comic or pathetic liabilities, obsessions, or enthusiasms plague the several characters in *Rasselas* (Imlac's passion for poetry, the prince's enthusiasm for seeing the world, the astronomer's obsession with his responsibility for the weather), these errors are at least predicated on imagined action. Such imagining, while not a sufficient condition for doing good, is at least a necessary one.[10]

He now resumes the rhythms of understatement to describe how he actually composed the *Dictionary*, stating matter-of-factly that it was a substantial undertaking. Plain statement now replaces hyperbole:

---

10. Walter Jackson Bate emphasizes this point about the importance of action or movement of almost any kind over inaction in *The Achievement of Samuel Johnson*.

Having therefore no assistance but from general grammar, I applied myself to the perusal of our writers; and noting whatever might be of use to ascertain or illustrate any word or phrase, accumulated in time the materials of a dictionary, which, by degrees, I reduced to method, establishing to myself, in the progress of the work, such rules as experience and analogy suggested to me.

As he earlier condensed the melodramatic description of the lexicographer's woes into the single word *disappointments*, so he now refers to the massive project of reading for the *Dictionary* with similar economy. Thus he chooses to understate a task whose magnitude would seem difficult to overstate. Such, he now suggests a second time, are the operations of history upon memory. In prospect a project may appear either grandly heroic or sublimely gloomy. But once completed, it enters the past and takes on a quality of matter-of-factness, now becoming simply something done and thus separate from its maker's fantasies. Occupying a space not bounded by the imagination alone, actual achievement simplifies diction and resists hyperbole by measuring the ratio of our losses to our gains.

The stability resulting from this calculation does to some degree make up for the inevitable disappointment of comparing achievements with aims. The personal energy of the creator that characterizes a project's beginnings rechannels itself into a new identity of the maker, now become a critic of his own work, after the thing is made. From such thinking it follows that since different moods and personae characterize and occupy different stages of a project so, too, different styles must be invented to narrate those stages. The implications of such thinking for writing a biographical history of culture became one of Johnson's subjects in composing the *Lives of the Poets* (1777–1781).

The first three paragraphs, then, introduce the author and his history in the project. Not simply in their subject matter, but in their rhythms as well, they reenact the qualities of the author's mind engaging his work. At this deep level of rhythms Johnson most effectively educates his reader. These rhythms, rather than the subject matter as such, constitute the deliberately biographical nature of this preface, which Cyril H. Knoblauch has called "the autobiography of a book."[11] Johnson's Preface makes his dictionary

11. On this point see also Leo Braudy's "Lexicography and Biography in the *Preface* to Johnson's *Dictionary*," especially his comments about the power of the argument and about the complex interrelation "between procedural prob-

visible in the same way his introduction to Baretti's *Guide Through the Royal Academy* brings the paintings into view before the reader actually sees them. It makes the *Dictionary* visible as an object with a history (an account of the author's perceptions, insights, decisions, uncertainties, and disappointments); with a present (its structure and use); and with a future (its continuing use and the invitation made by its flaws and incompleteness for corrections and improvements). As the *Dictionary* itself makes language visible as an object of study, so the Preface makes the *Dictionary* visible. In both instances, what was formerly on the margins of consciousness becomes focal.[12]

Such a reorientation has several effects. Perhaps most significantly it destabilizes the book as a monolithic form, displaying its parts and segments both in time and space from several points of view. In addition, it demonstrates how the book has dimension, dramatic texture, and density—qualities that do not belong to the object as such and that would not be self-evident to the unacquainted observer but that become apparent to anyone acquainted with the history of its composition.[13] Everyone, Johnson believed, is interested in knowing how things came to be the way they are now. Tapping this interest, a writer engages the reader's imaginative participation in learning. Acquainting the reader genetically with the dictionary's composition, the Preface gives strategic, practical knowledge for using this book in comprehensive and comprehending ways.

Such knowledge by acquaintance makes the difference between a reader's feeling competent and feeling incompetent to use a book. While the precise difference between these two feelings is difficult to specify, we all know from experience the functional difference between the two. The Preface is thus more than substantively informative. It also empowers the reader with a conceptual and emotional attitude toward the work. One of the chief qualities of knowledge by acquaintance is the kind of practical and pervasive confidence it evokes in us. The assets of such knowledge are nonetheless real for being general rather than particular. One need only

---

lems in the making of the *Dictionary* and personal problems in Johnson's own life" (552).

12. Polanyi elaborates this distinction in *Personal Knowledge*, 88, 92, 115.

13. A substantial account of this history of composition appears in James H. Sledd and Gwin J. Kolb, eds., *Dr. Johnson's Dictionary: Essays in the Biography of a Book.*

consult other the experience of reading other writers' prefaces to recognize Johnson's distinctive accomplishment in communicating useful information.

WHAT OTHERS COULD DO IF THEY TOOK THE TIME

A lawyer, Johnson once observed, does for people what they could do for themselves if they took the time to study law. My reading of the Preface to the *Dictionary* implies that the same might be said of the lexicographer. He characterizes the making of the dictionary as an undertaking that, while burdensome, is neither impossible nor even fundamentally unfamiliar, even to those who have never done such work. Familiarizing us with his work, giving us an insider's knowledge, he acquaints us with the work, including its history. And this phenomenon of acquaintance encourages our using the *Dictionary.*

Informing readers about how and why he did what he did, he also, from time to time, invites their judgment of his success. This invitation, in turn, reinforces one of the themes of the Preface: "In examining the orthography of any doubtful word, the mode of spelling by which it is inserted in the series of the dictionary, is to be considered as that to which I give, perhaps, not often rashly, the preference. I have left, in the examples, to every author his own practice unmolested, that the *reader may balance suffrages, and judge betwixt us"* (emphasis mine). We are all, in varying degrees, qualified to judge a lexicographer's decisions because his problems, solutions, and explanations derive basically from our common experience of using the language. It is the lexicographer's consciousness about language and his task, less than his experience as such, that distinguishes him from other people.

To say that consciousness is the principal distinguishing quality of the dictionary maker's professionalism is not, of course, to say that consciousness alone promises accurate judgments about language. Jonathan Swift, a conscious lexicographer if ever there was one, made the radically faulty demand that no words "should be suffered to become obsolete." His demand mistook the meaning of the word *obsolete*, interpreting obsolescence to mean a willed and hence controllable condition. According to Johnson, Swift fundamentally misunderstood the relationship between language and life, between words and their use. The manner in which he identifies Swift's error illuminates his own presuppositions and methods: "But what makes a word obsolete, more than general agreement to forbear it? and how shall it be continued, when it conveys an offensive idea, or recalled again into the mouths of mankind, when it has once by disuse become unfamiliar, and by unfamiliarity unpleasing?" Dictionary makers typically hope to preserve the language they compile, if in part because they need to imagine a heroic outcome to sustain their labor. But if this ideal is taken literally, rather than used figuratively to motivate the work, it becomes both an inaccurate guide and evidence of the writer's being lost in lexicography.

The danger of becoming lost in one's subject is the obverse of those healthy qualities of curiosity, dedication, and hope necessary to any significant undertaking. This danger threatens readers as well. They, too, may become lost in their work of judgment by taking literally the ideals that should figuratively guide their judgment. To prevent this error of literalism readers must, from time to time, attempt to imagine books from their authors' points of view and consider how

> things, equally easy in themselves, are not all equally easy to any single mind. Every writer of a long work commits errours, where there appears neither ambiguity to mislead, nor obscurity to confound him; and in a search like this, many felicities of expression will be casually overlooked, many convenient parallels will be forgotten, and many particulars will admit improvement from a mind utterly unequal to the whole performance.

Any particular mind has its own peculiar limitations that may not affect another mind, though that second mind will have its own failings equally puzzling to the first. Johnson's apology, by offering details that permit us to imagine the mind of another, goes beyond the usual function of such writing. His analysis of this condition of difference introduces biographical thinking into the activity of making critical judgments.

His aim in distinguishing between two kinds of minds (one that "will admit improvement" but is "unequal to the whole performance" and one that, although it may fail on a number of individual counts, proves itself equal to an entire performance) is to identify the kind of undertaking a dictionary represents. The project becomes visible through descriptions of the distinctive effort and skill required to perform it and the characteristic errors and flaws it can absorb without seriously damaging the whole. Even work conventionally thought of as impersonal and objective, like a dictionary, bears the distinctive marks of its composer's mind.

There is no such thing as impersonal work. By making the dictionary once again visible as artifact, this time in terms of its creation as the work of an individual, Johnson also aims to place this work in a specific autobiographical and epistemological context. The Preface educates the reader on the subject of how at issue in composing a dictionary are not mere technical or procedural skills but issues of perception, epistemology, and identity.

His comments about how different minds are qualified for different undertakings also clear the way of potential critics. He makes these remarks not only to defend himself, but also to make way for his severest and best-informed critic, namely himself:

> I have not always executed my own scheme, or satisfied my own expectations. The work, whatever proofs of diligence and attention it may exhibit, is yet capable of many improvements: the orthography which I recommend is still controvertible; the etymology which I adopt is uncertain, and perhaps frequently erroneous; the explanations are sometimes too much contracted, and sometimes too much diffused, the significations are distinguished rather with subtilty than skill, and the attention is harrassed with unnecessary minuteness.

Simplicity of diction and syntax again characterizes Johnson's historical assessment of his accomplishment.

These remarks, in turn, introduce his discussion of the psychology of achievement: "To rest below his own aim is incident to every one whose fancy is active, and whose views are comprehensive; nor is any man satisfied with himself, because he has done much, but because he can conceive little." Active fancy and comprehensive views are practical assets. They motivate patient, hard work, but they also carry the liability of almost certain disappointment. Satisfaction, by contrast, is generally the mark of contracted views. He whose active fancy dreamed the persona of the poet not merely to aggrandize but also to direct his work found himself instead "doomed at last to wake a lexicographer." Such a discovery is in part a fated disappointment. But this disappointment also takes the measure of talent and will—the talent to imagine more than one can accomplish, the will to continue despite disappointment and to determine the time to conclude, however inconclusively.

This psychological pattern of achievement that Johnson discerned in the nearly ten years of working on the *Dictionary* he later elaborated in the plot of *Rasselas*. Here, too, he dramatizes the importance of knowing when to end a project and of acting on that knowledge by "determining to desist." The decision to stop working on the *Dictionary,* like the travelers' decision to end their journey in *Rasselas,* requires the intelligence to review one's original motives and aims and to attempt to see that work from a new historical perspective, looking backward and forward simultaneously. This different angle involves looking *at* the inquiry itself rather than simply pursuing it. Viewing the *Dictionary* in this way, Johnson reports that he "saw that one enquiry only gave occasion to another, that book referred to book, that to search was not always to find, and to find was not always to be informed." This sense of an ending involves disappointment and the perception of one's limitations. But it also gives evidence of a healthy and hopeful mind. The capacities to accept disappointment and to choose its time, to aim high while knowing that one must conclude inconclusively, are signs of mature thinking.

Such a model of thinking makes change identical with hope, as well as with the active workings of the imagination.[14] The importance of this discovery lies chiefly in the way the discovery itself enacts a kind of genius all too easily overlooked—genius erupting in the midst of the ordinary and reimagining what it sees. Critics have underscored Johnson's sublime melancholy in the Preface, the grandeur of his irony, his earnestness, and disappointment, all of which are present. But the Preface also, and perhaps more significantly, gives an account of how a writer invented different forms of wishing appropriate to the several stages of his project. It is thereby an argument on behalf of the importance of such inventiveness in the creative process.

THE GOOD WRITER

In their readings of the Preface to the *Dictionary,* as in other of his work, critics have often emphasized its heroic aspects. Perhaps it is time to make a case for its practical goodness—*goodness* used here in the sense that Charles M. Fair defines it in *The Dying Self.*[15] Fair defines this concept to include being organized, having one's powers available, seeing things whole, knowing when to change direction. When old ways of thinking or desire or habit fail,

14. In *Images of Faith: An Exploration of the Ironic Imagination,* William F. Lynch identifies hope with the very possibility of change. He also discusses hope as the opposite of boredom in chapter 4, "The Images of Faith and Human Time."

15. *The Dying Self,* 202.

good people invent new ones. In these ways Johnson was organized and hence, by this definition, good.

Such revisions are significant expressions of creativity and of hope, particularly so in the way Johnson does not make the common error of simplistically renouncing his former ways in order either to justify a new direction or to save face. He understood the importance of not denying two things at once, because he knew that for negation to succeed it must remain connected with previous affirmations and training.[16] Only when negation succeeds in this way can past experience serve as a resource for future knowledge, thus enabling us to think well by projecting our past ways of knowing into a future we can justly claim as our own. The dictionary maker may have to abandon certain aims or methods along the way, as for instance his aim of choosing illustrative citations that would accumulate into a conduct book and history of ideas. But, having failed at this undertaking because he had to edit many of the citations or quote them misleadingly out of context, he does not thereby renounce or undervalue that aim. It remains a stated ideal, preserved in the text and thus alive as an imaginative possibility of his own creative past and perhaps of another author's future.

As in hope there is a principle of adaptability, so in reliable thinking there is a principle of economy. This economy allows us to keep what we have replaced and does not require a denial for each new assertion. The familiar passage where Johnson defends himself against the possible charge of becoming lost in lexicography illustrates this principle of economy:

> I am not yet so lost in lexicography, as to forget that *words are the daughters of earth, and that things are the sons of heaven.* Language is only the instrument of science, and words are but the signs of ideas: I wish, however, that the instrument might be less apt to decay, and that signs might be permanent, like the things which they denote.

This passage summarizes the older metaphoric view and the newer scientific one of language,[17] first constructing a miniature mythol-

16. Gaston Bachelard, *The Philosophy of No: A Philosophy of the New Scientific Mind*, 117.

17. William K. Wimsatt, Jr., in "Johnson's Dictionary," observes that there was a "certain special relation between metaphor and science . . . during the age of Johnson" and that "many of the most novel and ample opportunities for metaphor arose during this period out of the very words by which science was altering the known contours of ordinary physical reality and the trend of any educated man's thoughts about that reality" (89).

ogy to distinguish words from things, then placing this conception side by side with the newer scientific view of language as instrumental or semiotic. Each depiction satisfies different imaginative and philosophical needs and desires: the one lyrical and associative, the other rational and analytic. He renounces neither.

The preceding observations are, in turn, related to Johnson's understanding of the ways a dictionary should open out onto the language rather than attempt to enclose it by definition. Definition assumes language as artifact rather than as the medium in and through which we live. His desire, shared with Swift, to conserve language imagines a very different scene of its use from his predecessor:

> I shall not think my employment useless or ignoble, if by my assistance foreign nations, and distant ages, gain access to the propagators of knowledge, and understand the teachers of truth; if my labours afford light to the repositories of science, and add celebrity to *Bacon*, to *Hooker*, to *Milton*, and to *Boyle*.
>
> When I am animated by this wish, I look with pleasure on my book, however defective, and deliver it to the world with the spirit of a man that has endeavoured well.

The lexicographer's activities as an agent in culture and as an intermediary in the history of reading acknowledge the implications of this view of language as a force in culture. Combined with the way Johnson composed the *Dictionary*, by first reading primary sources in literature from which he selected illustrative passages, these details demonstrate how acutely he understood the relationship between literature and lexicography. Literature, he perceived, is of greater use to those who make and those who use dictionaries than are dictionaries to those who read and write literature.[18] A dictionary may, in some limited way, help us read a poem. But the reverse is more largely true. By reading many poems we learn how to use a dictionary. Johnson was well aware of the fact that meaning is an occurrence; it is use. At the same time that a dictionary systematizes language, it also becomes another instance of its use.

This awareness embodied in the *Dictionary* makes it an unusually and broadly useful book. It succeeds in large part because Johnson does not misunderstand a dictionary's particular varieties

18. Donald R. Howard makes this observation about how poems are of more use to dictionaries than dictionaries are to poems, in "Lexicography and the Silence of the Past," 15.

of usefulness. His wish to enable future generations to read past writers is based on this perception of how lexicography, far from being a technical, rational, or abstract skill, takes its methods as well as its matter from life. It is a complex and intermingled drama. To this perception and its implications for literature he returned ten years later in the *Preface to Shakespeare* (1765).

EARNING OUR INHERITANCE:
THE *PREFACE TO SHAKESPEARE*

In this later preface Johnson elaborates the *Dictionary*'s emphasis on the reader and reading from additional points of view. He considers the reader's psychology, along with the politics of the relationship between reader and writer. The latter, an issue earlier identified in the preface to *The Preceptor*, is addressed in the following passage from his Preface to Shakespeare's plays:

> The reader, I believe, is seldom pleased to find his opinion anticipated; it is natural to delight more in what we find or make, than in what we receive. Judgement, like other faculties, is improved by practice, and its advancement is hindered by submission to dictatorial decisions, as the memory grows torpid by the use of a table book. Some initiation is however necessary; of all skill, part is infused by precept, and part is obtained by habit; I have therefore shewn so much as may enable the candidate of criticism to discover the rest. (YJ 7:104)

Johnson knew the importance of pleasure in education. However useful its contents may be, a book that the reader lays aside is useless. Usefulness is not an inherent quality but an after-the-fact assessment. Because we take more pleasure "in what we find or make, than in what we receive," pleasure in reading depends largely on the reader's feeling that the writer recognizes and acknowledges the audience's participation, combining freedom and responsibility, in the text. Yet granted the pleasures and the educational value of independent thinking, there remains the necessity of "some initiation" since "of all skill, part is infused by precept, and part is obtained by habit." The writer of prefaces, like any other teacher, must walk a fine line between showing enough to "enable the candidate of criticism to discover the rest," on the one hand, and dictating too much, on the other.

These insights are grounded in an understanding that real learning is neither mere memorizing nor even mastery alone. Rather it consists of altering the student's perspective. Such alterations cannot be forgotten because they become part of the way we live. Neither are they, in the conventional sense, difficult because, having occurred, they seem self-evident. The kind of educational activity most interesting to Johnson cannot be adequately defined or assessed in terms of either memory or mastery, though they may include both. They are another order of experience. The familiar anecdote of the way he composed lengthy passages in his mind before putting words on paper gives a vivid picture of the man I have so far been describing:

> He, therefore, never composed what we call a foul draft on paper of any thing he published, but used to revolve the subject in his mind, and turn and form every period, till he had brought the whole to the highest correctness and the most perfect arrangement. Then his uncommonly retentive memory enabled him to deliver a whole essay, properly finished, whenever it was called for. The writer of this note has often heard him humming and forming periods, in low whispers to himself, when shallow observers thought he was muttering prayers, &c.[19]

As for Johnson the act of learning requires students to recompose knowledge in their own minds, so his own habit of composing—under his breath arranging, rearranging, until he had established the right order and right rhythms of his prose or poetry—embodies his belief that knowledge is something we must make our own in a personal drama of educational embodiment.

This anecdote also serves as prologue to my argument about the *Preface to Shakespeare*. From the notion of learning as a personal process of embodying knowledge in our lives there follows Johnson's practice of taking on several different roles in this process of reformation. In the *Dictionary*, for instance, he notes that he has proceeded with "a scholar's reverence for antiquity" and "a grammarian's regard for the genius of the language." These are but two of his several roles. He is also an intermediary between future readers and the authors of past ages, the failed poet, and finally an ordinary civilian, a participant in that collective enterprise we call culture and one who both uses the language and takes interest in its great writers.

The cross-connections among these roles and responsibilities imply deeply held beliefs on Johnson's part about how every inheritance must be earned anew (otherwise, alienation and demoraliza-

19. "Anecdotes and Remarks by Bishop Percy," in G. B. Hill, ed., *Johnsonian Miscellanies*, 2:215–16.

tion occur)[20] and also about how understanding is not a single or unitary experience but a manifold and multiform activity.[21] To inherit the past authentically always involves translating that past into present terms. We do not find the past; we make it. And this process is perennial, never completed as long as we live. It is coincidental with life itself.

He opens this preface with just such an exercise in recomposing our inheritance by exposing a perverse but not uncommon assessment of the past:

> That praises are without reason lavished on the dead, and that the honours due only to excellence are paid to antiquity, is a complaint likely to be always continued by those, who, being able to add nothing to truth, hope for eminence from the heresies of paradox; or those, who, being forced by disappointment upon consolatory expedients, are willing to hope from posterity what the present age refuses, and flatter themselves that the regard which is yet denied by envy, will be at last bestowed by time. (YJ 7:59)

The diseconomy identified here is another example of the failure to understand the terms of our relationship with the past and the grounds of our orientation toward the future. Those who would on principle deny the excellence of the past also deny their own future for they are denying the hope of continuity.

True to his lexicographer's background, Johnson identifies the word *antiquity* as the central problem for consideration. The virtues of his mind are always, in part, the virtues of one whose assessment of any problem habitually includes consideration of the historical phenomena of language. Like Hegel, he recognizes that every condition of being is a *to have become*. The task Johnson now undertakes is to define the history of antiquity and to analyze the politics of its use. In considering the psychology and politics of praise, he asserts that the words *antiquity* and *the dead* are not neutrally referential. Each carries a political agenda. He understands that the conventions, definitions, and prejudices constituting things-as-they-are are historical phenomena. Further he knows that we owe it to ourselves to inquire historically into how things came to be the way they are. For him one of the crucial issues for reader and writer alike is less the anxiety of influence than the

20. Kenneth Burke, *Attitudes toward History*, 246.
21. Ludwig Wittgenstein proposes the notion of understanding as a family of experiences in *The Blue and Brown Books: Preliminary Studies for the "Philosophical Investigations."*

problem of how to prevent the narrowing and rigidifying effects of merely self-interested thinking.

These effects are often most clearly visible in a vocabulary of inert, because unexamined, terms: "Antiquity, like every other quality that attracts the notice of mankind, has undoubtedly votaries that reverence it, not from reason, but from prejudice" (YJ 7:59). The earlier passage demonstrates that antiquity is not something in and of the past but rather a name given to certain kinds of evaluations made of that past. This term identifies a behavior toward history that expresses itself in hopes, fears, praise, and blame. Antiquity, then, is not some *thing* or even some *time*, but a quality that we identify in or attribute to people and to what they have done. This distinction is no small one. It is crucial to Johnson's project of dematerializing and destabilizing the notion of antiquity, thereby to revitalize its meaning and usefulness.

This done, he now proceeds to substantiate and stabilize his method of inquiry: "Demonstration immediately displays its power, and has nothing to hope or fear from the flux of years; but works tentative and experimental must be estimated by their proportion to the general and collective ability of man, as it is discovered in a long succession of endeavours" (YJ 7:60). Johnson takes the cue for his method of investigation (by comparison and estimation) from the object he is investigating ("works tentative and experimental"). He adopts the operations of probability to assess "the general and collective ability of man" as it is discovered in "a long succession of endeavours."

First dematerializing the conventional sense of the past, then quantifying his methods for examining that past, he introduces the notion of an immaterial real soon to be applied to his reading of Shakespeare, specifically to explain how the poet earns our belief: "If there be any fallacy, it is not that we fancy the players, but that we fancy ourselves unhappy for a moment; but we *rather lament the possibility than suppose the presence of misery, as a mother weeps over her babe, when she remembers that death may take it from her*" (YJ 7:78, emphasis mine). The passage makes a case for dramatic reality being a perceptually complex experience, emotionally moving precisely by virtue of its being removed. The reality of emotion in drama functions at two removes from action. But it is nonetheless powerful by virtue of this fact. Indeed, thanks to this distinction and the leverage it supplies, emotion in drama is all the more powerful. Johnson's proposal also enlarges our view of what is real and thereby of consequence. It further illustrates how an accurate psychological analysis of the way drama affects the reader in no way lessens its emotional force. When the audience sees a mother weep over her dead child, it laments this possibility for itself, rather than mistakes the actor's portrayal of grief for real grief. To recognize this fact equips the reader to be affected by drama in a more powerful, not less powerful, way by bringing the structuring force of imagination to the aid of emotion.

In a similar way he cross-examines conventional notions of chronology in history when he comments on our and Shakespeare's mutual debt, inviting us to imagine what can be gained by thinking about time in new ways.[22] Here is a different perspective on the act of reading: "Yet it must be at last confessed, that as we owe every thing to him, he owes something to us; that, if much of his praise is paid by perception and judgement, much is likewise given by custom and veneration" (YJ 7:91). The debt between a dead author and future readers is also mutual. They collaborate in creating one another. By withholding Shakespeare's name until several paragraphs into the *Preface*, Johnson freshens the reader's attention to consider the issue of the playwright's reputation with renewed and independent energy: "The poet, of whose works I have undertaken the revision, may now begin to assume the dignity of an ancient, and claim the privilege of established fame and prescriptive veneration" (YJ 7:61). He is now unquestionably an ancient. But this general and accurate attitude toward him does not preclude rethinking assessments of his work. Indeed, it may make such rethinking all the more challenging and necessary.

As Johnson reconceives the notion of antiquity into a concept that measures and evaluates rather than names inherent qualities, so he subsequently recasts this revisionary definition by locating it within a larger, more encompassing activity. This larger activity takes its inspiration and form from the mind's natural curiosity about the creative process:

> Every man's performances, to be rightly estimated, must be compared with the state of the age in which he lived, and with his own particular opportunities; and though to the reader a book be not worse or better for the circumstances of the authour, yet as there is always a silent reference of human works to human abilities, and as the enquiry, how

22. Paul K. Alkon discusses time in relation to the reader and the act of reading in "Johnson and Chronology."

far man may extend his designs, or how high he may rate his native force, is of far greater dignity than in what rank we shall place any particular performance, curiosity is always busy to discover the instruments, as well as to survey the workmanship, to know how much is to be ascribed to original powers, and how much to casual and adventitious help. (YJ 7:81)

Assessment or ranking is here presented as a subcategory of the impulse to compare "human works to human abilities," a broadly fascinating activity in which everyone is more or less qualified to participate. The significance and scope of such evaluations are measured in direct proportion to the commonly distributed resources of interest and skill brought to bear in making them. Criticism is a subspecies of general human curiosity.

By suggesting that the highest and most dignified critical act is one that all of us are, in varying degrees, qualified to perform and by locating the activity of criticism within a broader context than that of reading alone, Johnson reasserts, this time with regard to the critic, the notion earlier asserted about the lexicographer. Each performs a practical, unmysterious, and not very difficult service. Neither should ever assert otherwise because to do so would fundamentally mislead readers about the nature of the task and their function in it. The critic's chief responsibility is to place reading in a larger context than the merely literary. Thus the primary challenge posed to those of us among Johnson's readers who are literary critics is to remain alert to his premises about the larger contextualizing duties of the critical imagination.[23]

The context of reading, then, extends throughout the culture for the simple reason that major works of literature, like major scientific achievements, alter the ways people think and thus also the ways they behave. The changing intellectual and behavioral condi-

23. On the question of difficulty in the preface to *Shakespeare*, Donald T. Siebert, Jr., argues that Johnson consciously increases our difficulties in "The Scholar as Satirist: Johnson's Edition of Shakespeare." Siebert observes that he "manipulates us as readers: as Johnson seesaws back and forth from one position to its apparent opposite, we begin to lose confidence in our ability to understand exactly where Johnson does stand or to predict what he will finally say. But as somewhat helpless readers we have to rely on Johnson to bring us out of our confusion" (493). Patrick O'Flaherty in remarks about the *Rambler* that could be well applied to the preface to *Shakespeare* makes a convincing reply to this contention: "When Johnson thought he knew the truth, he told the truth as directly as he could" ("Towards an Understanding of Johnson's *Rambler*," 525).

tions of a culture, as those changes result in part from any new performance of genius, fascinated Johnson both for the evidence they offer of the force of art and for the explanation they give of the profound urge we feel toward learning. Perhaps they are also central to the definition of our humanity. Shakespeare educated a nation. He did not set out explicitly to teach, but from him a nation learned. As precisely as Johnson recognized all the difficulties and odds against successful education, so he also perceived, to borrow Carl L. Becker's wittily serious observation, that you can't count on people not learning.[24] The impulse to learn is deeply rooted.

Johnson's depiction of Shakespeare's circumstances and the characteristics of his world, when he began writing his plays, illustrates this point:

> But the greater part of his excellence was the product of his own genius. He found the English stage in a state of the utmost rudeness; no essays either in tragedy or comedy had appeared, from which it could be discovered to what degree of delight either one or other might be carried. Neither character nor dialogue were yet understood. Shakespeare may be truly said to have introduced them both amongst us, and in some of his happier scenes to have carried them both to the utmost height. (YJ 7:87)

The poet found the English stage in one condition and left it in another. Writing both tragedy and comedy, introducing character and dialogue whose excellence educated his public in the "degree of delight" to which "they might be carried," he could scarcely have predicted the many ways his work would educate a nation. This unpredictable quality by which a work alters future expectations characterizes the mind and work of the genius. It also ironically explains why geniuses are often forgotten. Years later in his *Life of Dryden* Johnson noted how eighteenth-century readers of Dryden's *Essay of Dramatick Poesie* (1668) had difficulty imagining a time before this writer's critical concepts existed, so profoundly and "naturally" had they shaped a culture's thinking. In becoming part of the way we think and perceive, the changes that they inspire come to seem so natural and inevitable that we forget their origin. Part of the critic's job, as Johnson was to examine at length in the *Lives of the Poets*, is to counteract this oblivion.

In the Preface to the *Dictionary* Johnson subordinates the pur-

24. "*What Is the Good of History?*" *Selected Letters of Carl L. Becker, 1900–1945*, 320.

pose of the essay and his role as guardian of the language to the larger aim of mediating between past writers and future readers. So, too, in this later preface he subordinates the critic's activity of ranking Shakespeare and of measuring his achievement to his function as a mediator between the work and the reader. These critical activities are aspects of a characteristic behavior on his part, as he alternates between materializing and dematerializing his subject matter, displacing and repositioning topics. These alternations give force to his assertion about the economy of criticism as it analyzes the gains and losses experienced over time in the cultural investment of reading and in the drama of scholarship and criticism that is even more volatile and, on the whole, less efficient and economical:

> It is no pleasure to me, in revising my volumes, to observe how much paper is wasted in confutation. Whoever considers the revolutions of learning, and the various questions of greater or less importance, upon which wit and reason have exercised their powers, must lament the unsuccessfulness of enquiry, and the slow advances of truth, when he reflects, that great part of the labour of every writer is only the destruction of those that went before him. The first care of the builder of a new system, is to demolish the fabricks which are standing. . . . The opinions prevalent in one age, as truths above the reach of controversy, are confuted and rejected in another, and rise again to reception in remoter times. Thus the human mind is kept in motion without progress. Thus sometimes truth and errour, and sometimes contrarieties of errour, take each others place by reciprocal invasion. The tide of seeming knowledge which is poured over one generation, retires and leaves another naked and barren; the sudden meteors of intelligence which for a while appear to shoot their beams into the regions of obscurity, on a sudden withdraw their lustre, and leave mortals again to grope their way. (YJ 7:99)

The metaphors of cultural and natural wastefulness, of motion without progress, and of purposeless repetition depict a condition of similarly wasteful thinking. This portrait argues the case that, while the best criticism and scholarship may have their real uses, Shakespeare remains a better investment than his critics, because he is more lasting. And since, as finite beings, our principal moral resource is time and our chief responsibility is to use it well, the issue of our relationship to Shakespeare involves more than merely literary considerations.

The other side of diseconomy in criticism is false productivity. While their forms are different, their effects are the same. The activity of writing critical and scholarly notes, for instance, is simple enough. And the genre itself practically ensures the author's success:

> The work is performed, first by railing at the stupidity, negligence, ignorance, and asinine tastelessness of the former editors, and shewing, from all that goes before and all that follows, the inelegance and absurdity of the old reading; then by proposing something, which to superficial readers would seem specious, but which the editor rejects with indignation; then by producing the true reading, with a long paraphrase, and concluding with loud acclamations on the discovery, and a sober wish for the advancement and prosperity of genuine criticism. (YJ 7:108)

While he admits that "all this may be done, and perhaps done sometimes without impropriety," he adds his suspicion that "the reading is right, which requires many words to prove it wrong; and the emendation wrong, that cannot without so much labour appear to be right. The justness of a happy restoration strikes at once" (YJ 7:108-9). Good scholarship, like all successful problem-solving, is economical. In two late works, *A Journey to the Western Islands* (1775) and the *Lives of the Poets* (1779-1781), the subjects of Chapters 5 and 6 respectively, Johnson returned once again to these issues.

SAVING TIME

The ideal of using time well is the principal theme of the *Preface to Shakespeare*. Thus it follows that the question of Shakespeare's failure to observe the unity of time becomes the central symbolic consideration of the essay. Just as Johnson revised the word *antiquity*, so in his discussion of time, he similarly reconsiders the term: "Time is, of all modes of existence, most obsequious to the imagination; a lapse of years is as easily conceived as a passage of hours" (YJ 7:78). Critics who have faulted Shakespeare for abusing the unity of time present themselves as guardians of refinement and accuracy at war with a writer whose work is unrefined and careless. Johnson argues that such notions of refinement may appeal to reason but are in reality much more farfetched, because literal-minded, than the supposed faults they identify. Yet more significantly, these critics fail to grapple with the full and fascinating difficulty confronting any reader of drama: What constitutes our belief in drama? And how does drama function if it is not credited? He makes a tautological reply simple in form only: "It is credited with all the credit due to the drama." His deliberate circularity identifies the profound fact about all arts and sciences, namely that they operate by their own indigenous terms, which serve, in turn, as the basis for examining them.

The same theory of economy directs Johnson's advice about how to use his work. Readers as yet *unacquainted* with Shakespeare's powers should

> read every play from the first scene to the last, with utter negligence of all his commentators. . . . Particular passages are cleared by notes, but the general effect of the work is weakened. The mind is refrigerated by interruption; the thoughts are diverted from the principal subject; the reader is weary, he suspects not why; and at last throws away the book, which he has too diligently studied. (YJ 7:111)

Overdependence on the critic interrupts the reader's primary relationship with the writer, fatigues her, is in short, mistaken. Critics who mistake their place in the reading process fail to understand that their primary responsibility is a negative one. They should at the very least not weaken the text. They should place no obstacles between the reader and the writing. Yet there are many temptations to do so, which all center around the critic's desire to be seen. Hence the reason for Johnson's assessment of notes as evils, however necessary they may be.

Thus it follows that when we begin to read, we should trust ourselves first to make the author's acquaintance. The force of confidence moves us forward, evidence of freedom and token of responsibility to think and act for ourselves. Such confidence is also grounds for a corresponding humility based on recognizing ourselves each to be one among many, part of a collective enterprise of thinking and acting of which literature is, if but a part, a significant part.

3

WRITING IN TIME

The *Rambler*

WHAT THE *RAMBLER* OFFERED TO ITS AUTHOR

By 1750, four years after Johnson had begun the *Dictionary*, he needed money. He also needed the "relief," as he called it, of writing short pieces to a different rhythm of deadlines than the single monumental one posed by this project.[1] The *Rambler* answered both needs, although like most imagined satisfactions it became, when achieved, its own special kind of problem. Writing to deadline became wearisome. But over time the *Rambler* also satisfied him for several lasting reasons expressed in his well-known assessment: "My other works are wine and water; but my *Rambler* is pure wine." Elizabeth Johnson, whose opinion mattered to her husband, also admired these essays: "I thought very well of you before; but I did not imagine you could have written any thing equal to this."[2] The *Rambler* was thus for its author a significant project in many different ways. By the time he decided to end the series two years later in 1752, he had written over two hundred essays. Apparently he was ready to stop. Yet only one year later he returned to essay writing as a contributor to the *Adventurer* (1753–1754) and, four years after that, to the *Idler* (1758–1760). These returns to the essay form invite speculation on their meaning to the author. Are they the triumph of hope over experience, the recollection of work well done, the prospect of pleasure in reestablishing a conversation with his audience, or some combination of the three?

Along with the welcome promise of regular income, the *Ram-*

1. Fussell comments on how "the whole series of essays is inextricably bound up with his work on the *Dictionary*, from which it served as a twice-weekly respite, if that is the right word to describe a self-imposed disciplinary task" (*Samuel Johnson and the Life of Writing*, 150).
2. Boswell, *Life*, 1:210n1, 210.

bler with its Tuesday and Saturday deadlines, may have been desirable to Johnson for other reasons. By virtue of its serial publication, this work offered a sense of no-doubt-welcome finiteness. He could see the results in print immediately and could thereby maintain a regular connection with his readers. Perhaps, too, the series offered an ongoing occasion for using some of the massive reading that went into the *Dictionary*, for elaborating unhappily truncated aphorisms in a narrative context, and for placing old texts in a new literary setting. In the Preface to the *Dictionary* he expressed disappointment at having had to shorten or alter many of his chosen citations. Having selected them originally as much for their edifying sentiments as for their aptness in illustrating meaning, he regretted having to edit or alter them. The *Rambler* thus may have appealed to him as an opportunity to recover some of these losses.

Perhaps this project also offered its author a sense of the real and substantial day-to-dayness of his work, linking him, his reading, and his readers in a circuit of ongoing, active communication during the long promissory period of work on the *Dictionary*. His lexicographical work was no less real than the series, but its identity was for many years defined by deferral and expectation. The *Rambler*, by contrast, provided an occasion for another rhythm of writing that unfolded differently in time. As the chief characteristic of the *Dictionary* is mass and the way it fills space with a single, if complex, subject, language, so the *Rambler*'s predominant characteristic is the serial quality of its unfolding and accumulating over time. Hence it is no accident that time is the subject of the concluding essay. While the *Dictionary* recognizes the relationship between time and language, it aims to give an extensive, spatial account of the language that, by its breadth and by the accumulating force of its examples, aims to combat time with space. Although Johnson was scarcely naive about a dictionary's power to fix language in the eternal present, he at least hoped to help conserve it.

Such proposals as these about how the *Dictionary* and the *Rambler* may have served complementary functions for their author cannot be proved. But they are a probable construction of his creative process. This kind of imagining fascinated Johnson for he believed it to be a legitimate activity of biography as well as an essential critical instinct for living. The last chapter of this study, which examines the *Lives of the Poets*, will elaborate this belief in more detail. The aim of the present chapter is to examine the major, distinctive feature of the *Rambler*, namely the way it embodies

Johnson's notion of knowledge as personal, telic, and fundamentally related to time. While these aspects of the series have not gone unnoticed, neither has their full significance been explored. M. P. Follett has expressed this Johnsonian understanding of knowledge for our century: "Concepts can never be *presented* to me merely, they must be *knitted into the structure of my being*, and this can only be done through my own activity" (emphasis mine).[3] The collective implications of this notion of knowledge are a major theme of the *Rambler*.

JOHNSON IN THE *RAMBLER*

From the outset this series had a reputation for being difficult. It raised the stakes in the educational tradition of sociability and disarming ease that had characterized Addison's and Steele's earlier work in the *Tatler* (1709–1711) and *Spectator* (1711–1712).[4] Formal characteristics account in large part for the *Rambler*'s difficulty. Johnson's formidable rendering of the periodic sentence and the demands made by his "philosophic words" on the reader are well known and have been well examined.[5] But these are less the origins of the difficulties experienced by readers than their appearance, more their form than their source. Their origin lies instead in his construction of a new persona for the series. Comparatively remote and more sternly philosophical, his character was tinged with melancholy. And while his humor was no less adept than those of his predecessors, it was on the whole subtler and less self-promoting.

The series also soon became the work, among all of his writings, with which the author himself was most strongly identified by his readers. This identification, growing over the years, retains its currency in the twentieth century. Most readers, if asked to name a single work representative of Johnson, are likely to say the *Rambler*, taking their cue no doubt in part from his own remarks about what the series meant to him. We have come to believe that in these essays the quintessential Johnson speaks to us.[6] There is thus

3. This excerpt from Follett's *Creative Experience* is an epigraph to Marion Milner's *On Not Being Able to Paint*, xi.

4. For an important and convincing discussion of how we need to "reconsider Johnson's conception of this periodical" and become alert "to echoes of the actual world of the early 1750s in these essays," see James F. Woodruff's "Johnson's *Rambler* and Its Contemporary Context."

5. William K. Wimsatt, Jr., *Philosophic Words: A Study of Style and Meaning in the Rambler and Dictionary of Samuel Johnson.*

6. George S. Marr, *The Periodical Essayists of the Eighteenth Century,* 131.

a central paradox in the history of reading this series. Here is the real but distant Johnson, the man himself yet impersonalized.

The *Rambler's* unique combination of a difficulty that distances readers from and a personality that invites them into a certain intimacy with the author thus invites a reconsideration of the author's presence in these essays. A promising direction for such an inquiry may lie in giving further consideration to the *Dictionary* and the *Rambler* together. To think genetically about these two works as products of complementary aspects of their creator's intelligence allows certain traits of each to emerge more clearly. In addition to occupying space and time differently, each of these works helps define and dramatize the identity of the author in relation to the distinctive aims, problems, and solutions he proposes in each project. Johnson's primary aim in writing the *Dictionary* was to connect present and future readers with the great authors of the past and thus also to connect these readers with one another in a history of reading. Stretching backward from the present into the past and forward into the future of language, the *Dictionary* aims to ensure a relatively continuous history of reading or at least one in which the ruptures are not absolute.[7] The *Rambler* essays, by contrast, place their emphasis on the discontinuous yet cumulative condition of our existence, sometimes addressing this subject as announced topic, always alluding to it by their serial format.

Johnson is chiefly an intermediary in the *Dictionary*, while in the *Rambler* he is chiefly the thinking subject. As he probably to some degree calculated and to some degree discovered along the way, a writer's personal presence in his inquiry involves posing difficulties for and making demands on the reader. Paradoxically, a degree of philosophical difficulty results from becoming more personal. The *Dictionary*, by contrast, is far from remote. Despite its size, it is less formidable than the *Rambler*, not so much because Johnson was here laboring explicitly to be less difficult as because he was laboring to bring readers closer to those from whom they inherited their language. Intent as he was to raise the philosophical and lexicographical stakes established forty years earlier by Addison and Steele, he was surely deliberate in making the *Rambler* difficult. Identifying his deliberate aim of raising the cultural stakes

---

7. On the encyclopedic nature of Johnson's undertaking in the *Dictionary*, see Robert DeMaria, Jr., *Johnson's Dictionary and the Language of Learning*.

also helps us account for why this series is both more and less personal than his other work.

While the *Dictionary* surely embodies Johnson's thinking, this embodiment functions chiefly as a kind of transparency or medium for his subject matter. But in the *Rambler*, thinking itself is primary. Each essay has an announced topic, but its drama is the author thinking. This personal quality may have less to do with its possible autobiographical content or style than with the way these essays so thoroughly and distinctively embody their author's qualities of thought, equally emphasizing its characteristic coherence and discontinuities. For these reasons, then, this series is demanding, and for these reasons, too, Johnson especially valued it. Like his predecessor, Montaigne, he writes the essay explicitly as a drama of personal knowledge. Ultimately the series becomes an argument on behalf of knowledge as an experience of persons over time. By this definition, knowledge thus has an affinity with the serial publication of these essays and with the identity that results from this publication, at once discrete and cumulative.[8] The *Rambler* can be adequately described neither according to the Cartesian model, "I think therefore I am;" nor according to its Lockean reversal, "I am therefore I think." Rather it is the more complex drama of the intersection of will, opportunity, pleasure, and necessity in the activity of thinking.

Consider, for instance, the way Johnson introduces the series in *Rambler* 1. The essay defines its topic at the outset as the difficulty and dangers of the "first address." This difficulty is witnessed by characteristics of this genre, its "settled and regular forms of salutation which necessity has introduced into all languages" (YJ 3:3). His analysis of the psychology of literary conventions introduces one of the major topics of the series. The author's desire to please is a subspecies of the common urge to please, a desire, in turn, always accompanied by uneasiness, fear, and suspicion. These anxieties often express themselves in "the vain expedients of softening cen-

8. In a manner related to these remarks on Johnson's composing of the *Rambler* and personal knowledge, Knoblauch observes that "against this background of shaken confidence in the power of writing and in the authority of texts, Johnson's literary struggle to retrieve a classical ideal of 'the stability of truth' assumes extraordinary complexity" ("Coherence Betrayed," 241). Paul J. Korshin discusses the different perceptions of the series by contemporary and later audiences in "Johnson's *Rambler* and Its Audiences."

sure by apologies, or rousing attention by abruptness" (YJ 3:4). Beginnings are never simple.

Reading and writing in the *Rambler* are metonymies for all encounters in which we become aware that our identities have boundaries to which we give the names *self* and *other*. The twice-weekly serialized essay gives form to this fact of consciousness, which the epigraphs, drawn from other writers, underscore. In reading each *Rambler* the reader encounters at least three writers. The opening epigraphs divide into stages the reader's approach to the body of the essay and thereby encourage us to gather our thoughts and take a position before we encounter the essayist. Johnson believed in tallying one's own ideas on a subject before listening to someone else's. Whenever he saw the title of a book, he inventoried what he knew on the topic and imagined how he would write about it before consulting the other writer. Such active self-consciousness works to counteract the insecurity potentially so damaging to good thinking. Ideas are part of the company we keep with ourselves, and we must with equal vigor believe in and question them. "When a man cannot bear his own company there is something wrong" (YJ 3:27), Johnson writes in *Rambler* 5. So, too, for living with our ideas.

As we must be comfortable, if not complacent, in the company of our own ideas, so must we be able to imagine ourselves in the world with no other being "but God and ourselves" (YJ 3:157). Yet at the same time, Johnson argues in the fifth essay, "it ought to be the endeavour of every man to derive his reflections from the objects about him; for it is to no purpose that he alters his position, if his attention continues fixed to the same point" (YJ 3:28). The former, chiefly a spatial metaphor, characterizes the way we distinguish ourselves autobiographically. The latter, chiefly a temporal metaphor, characterizes the way we educate ourselves biographically. Their successful intersection in a rhythm of equilibrium is the practical secular aim of Johnson's moral writings and one of his chief interests in the *Rambler*.

Oliver Goldsmith once observed to his friend, in what was almost surely a well-intentioned comment on their long friendship, "We have travelled over one another's minds." Johnson sternly corrected him: "Sir, you have not travelled over *my* mind, I promise you." For him a spatial metaphor was inadequate to describe the mind and to suggest "the limitless process, limitless principle, limitless possibility, which he thought the mind should represent."[9] Mind for him, like life itself, was multi-dimensional, its variety a factor of time and of space. Yet at the same time it was self-evident. Mind can neither go without saying nor can its phenomena ever be fully expressed.

TELLING TIME IN THE *RAMBLER*

Like the twentieth-century philosopher and critic Marjorie Grene, Johnson perceived that it is "from our existence as temporal beings, as histories, that our nature derives its ambiguous unity."[10] This conception offers a satisfying alternative to the timeless and rational Cartesian dualism, not because it simplifies either aspect but because it demonstrates how and why these notions are insufficiently complex to account for what we experience. The *Rambler* examines these notions in and through time. The second essay proposes the ultimate reality of time, introducing a motif that recurs throughout the series, giving it direction and form. Typically, Johnson examines time from the perspective of action. Although grammatically a noun, it functions for him as a verb, since time is synonymous with lived time. It is both the condition and the principle of organization whose meaning is, in turn, defined by either success or failure. Success and failure are two of the fundamental ways we evaluate life. Indeed they are synonymous with life, the measure of its meaning as the result of our action. Time is a telic phenomenon, humanized by effort, objectified by achievement.

Just as time is synonymous with experience, so is thought synonymous with thinking and knowledge with knowing. The telic nature of our life in time is the defining quality of human existence. It distinguishes our condition as creatures whose "motions are gradual, and whose life is progressive," whose "powers are limited," and who thus must use means to attain ends "and intend first what he performs last" [YJ 3:10]. The importance of identifying time with action, achievement, and hence telos, is their collective depiction of how the elements of our existence are interrelatedly at

---

9. In "'*Idler*' No. 24," Rhodes observes: "It is unnecessary to decide, then, as Robert Voitle does, that Johnson's was a 'whole-hearted acceptance of the Lockean theory of knowledge,' or to wonder, as does Hagstrum, why Johnson, the empiricist, frequently seems rationalistic. Actually, Johnson was both 'at once' an empirical rationalist and a Cartesian Lockean because he found in the mind's energy a metaphysical significance only partially acknowledged by Descartes and wholly unrecognized by Locke" (21).

10. *The Knower and the Known*, 88–89.

stake. If this progressive nature of life implies the necessity of directing our view always ahead, there are, Johnson notes, dangers in "keeping our view too intent upon remote advantages." Yet few major projects would ever be undertaken "if we had not the power of magnifying the advantages which we persuade ourselves to expect from them" (YJ 3:11). Thus imagination is necessary to the telos of living out the implications of our temporality.

In *Rambler* 1 the author-persona worries about the form of his first address, illustrating the common anxiety about failing to please and the associated hope to glide imperceptibly into the consciousness of others, mask our separateness, and hide our divisions. Despite these hopes and fears, we remain separate beings in a world of other separate beings. This existential fact, perhaps the major source of chronic human fear, cannot be corrected because it is less a problem as such, though it certainly causes problems, than a condition of our being. In *Rambler* 2 Don Quixote is presented to illustrate another related aspect of the human condition. With his visions and visionary schemes he embodies one of the notable characteristics of our minds whose natural flights "are not from pleasure to pleasure, but from hope to hope" (YJ 3:10). While Johnson usually locates madness and mental health along a continuum, here he emphasizes Quixote's identity with ourselves. This identification takes the measure of Johnson's belief in how an understanding of time as telic and hence imaginative is central to any adequate account of life.

Rambler 2 concludes with a comment about what authors fear most, namely neglect. As the first essay expressed the fear of being seen and then analyzed the liabilities and assets of visibility, the second essay identifies and confesses the even greater dread of invisibility. One fear replaces another yet more encompassing one. If there is irony here, there is also the therapy of comic inventiveness that underwrites creativity. Johnson simulates the way we move into the future, a pattern described by the essay itself, reversing the proposition we have been entertaining and discovering in this reversal a motive for renewed thinking: We move by discovering "new motives of action, new excitements of fear, and allurements of desire" (YJ 3:10). The essay thus enacts a convincing case for its advice.[11] Each *Rambler* also makes a yet more compelling case for

---

11. Leopold J. Damrosch, Jr., in his essay "Johnson's Manner of Proceeding in the *Rambler*" argues that his "method is to begin with a direct statement of

itself, one that criticism and scholarship by their nature and method are generally ill-equipped to identify. This case is one of time, not subject matter, and it resides in the intervening time between the publication of each essay, an interval of lived time for the reader and one that provides an enlarged and complicated context for the encounter with each essay.

Some of Johnson's familiar remarks about the relationship between reading and living allow us to imagine some of the ways, imprecisely calculable but nonetheless real, that he might have conceived the *Rambler*'s periodic publication intersecting the reader's lifetime. Reading, he thought, should always *fit into* life, in all senses of that phrase: "Books that you may carry to the fire, and hold readily in your hand," he commented, "are the most useful after all." In addition he remarked, "I would never desire a young man to neglect his business for the purpose of pursuing his studies, because it is unreasonable; I would only desire him to read a book during those hours when he would otherwise be unemployed."[12] His friends, too, commented on his characteristic interest in literature's fitting into life. William Seward remarked, for instance, that "Johnson was of the opinion that the happiest, as well as the most virtuous, persons were to be found amongst those who united with a business or profession a love of literature."[13] Hester Thrale noted that he "had never, by his own account, been a close student, and used to advise young people never to be without a book in their pocket, to be read at bye-times when they had nothing else to do."[14] Thus for him life always predominates over literature because there is literally more of the former than the latter. Life occupies more time and space. Hence life calls the living more strongly to its side and asserts itself as the first critical principle to be reckoned with in any reading of literature. Professional readers of his work, those of us who read the *Rambler* essays in a way that displaces them from their interwoven and subordinate relationship

---

the commonplace in aphoristic form, and then at once to attack and dismantle it. At the end he has usually put it together again, but it is no longer what it was before" (78).

12. "Apothegms, Sentiments, Opinions, & Occasional Reflections," in Hill, ed., *Johnsonian Miscellanies*, 2:2, 9.

13. "Anecdotes by William Seward, F.R.S.," in Hill, ed., *Johnsonian Miscellanies*, 2:309.

14. "Anecdotes of the late Samuel Johnson, LL.D," by Hesther Lynch Piozzi, in Hill, ed., *Johnsonian Miscellanies*, 1:181.

with life, need especially to consider the significance of his attitude about literature's appropriate subordination.

Johnson was never afraid to ask questions about the relationship between literature and life, about the use of books as well as their limitations. He poses these questions knowing that, like all truly important questions, they can never be finally settled yet must be asked repeatedly. Perhaps more than any other single expression of his thinking, the presence of such questions as these, which writing typically represses, accounts for his greatest value as a writer. He neither under- nor overvalues writing; he never mistakes how much self-opposition writing can absorb and can even turn to its own advantage. Thus he makes possible the construction of a compelling and valid case for writing by not arguing a mistaken case for its importance. Such a criterion may seem minimal for a convincing argument. Yet it is no common achievement. Just as Johnson argues that we serve great writers badly if we only appreciate their achievements and fail to identify their faults, so he also proposes that we undermine the force of literature by mistaking its relation and application to life.

WHAT THE *RAMBLER* DOES

From the vantage point of the foregoing comments, the twice-weekly appearance of the *Rambler* can be seen to take on a distinctive meaning in relation to the reader. These essays were written to intersect our lives and our lifetime in such a way as to enact Johnson's search for an alternative model of truth and hence of education to the conventional model based on cause and effect. The *Dictionary* by its monumentality emphatically asserts its presence, while the *Rambler* enters our lives with modest and brief regularity, fitting itself into whatever unemployed moments the reader may assign to it. An essay series thus seems to offer an ideal form to embody the appropriate subordinate function of literature, a function so defined by the way it withdraws our attention from life only briefly.

Yet however much literature must finally cede to life, however brief and subordinate should be our withdrawal from life to books, reading does serve a crucial need for Johnson, "while we continue in this complicated state" (YJ 3:97). As long as we must regulate "one part of our composition by some regard to the other" (YJ 3:97), books are of use if only to demonstrate the greater importance of life. But if the subordination of literature to life is for him a simple truth, its implications for reading and writing are as complex as life itself. As dictionaries are only truly useful to those who already know a language, so literature is most useful to those who know something about life. Its didactic function, based on its imitating life, is thus not linear, moving the reader from ignorance to knowledge along a straight line. Literature is both temporally and topologically complex in its educational routes.

The familiar anecdote of Johnson's replying to Bishop Berkeley's idealism by "striking his foot with mighty force against a large stone, *till he rebounded from it,* 'I refute it *thus*' "[15] (emphasis mine), depicts another way of considering the matter. The anecdote is a moving picture of Johnson's model of the relationship between self and world. His notion here dramatized is a view of the basic, stubborn, energizing recalcitrance of the world from which we sometimes quite literally rebound. It is for this reason that he recommends as the advantages of "vehemence and activity, that they are always hastening to their own reformation; because they incite us to try whether our expectations are well grounded, and therefore detect the deceits which they are apt to occasion" (YJ 3:138). A message sent returns in the form of a reply whose terms are not our own and must be translated.[16]

From this objectivity our subjectivity takes its meaning, and vice versa. The stone kicked until the one who kicks rebounds from it becomes a deep and invaluable resource of the self. It represents the world of alternatives, the all-that-we-are-not, which helps make us real. And yet the drama is more complicated even than this. When we kick the stone and rebound from it, we discover not only that there are objects outside ourselves but also that our subjectivity is, when viewed from another angle, objectivity. In the sequence of acts constituting this small but important drama, the actor alternates roles, first as subject (when kicking the stone), then as object (when rebounding from it). The distinctions are clear at any single moment. But over time the causes and effects alternate. They change positions so that no single account, based on their momentary positions, is adequate to the phenomena. This episode illus-

---

15. Boswell, *Life*, 1:471.

16. See H. F. Hallett's "Dr. Johnson's Refutation of Bishop Berkeley" for a discussion of the subtleties of Johnson's action. Lawrence J. Lipking considers this issue in the larger context of a suggestive discussion of the way "the opposition between books and life strikes Johnson with a force that writing cannot contain" ("Johnson and the Meaning of Life," 18).

trating Johnson's insight into how causal logic cannot fully account for and organize the world implies the necessity of seeking out alternative explanatory models. As the *Rambler*'s periodic intersection with the reader's life represents one alternative to this inadequate model, so the drama of conversation and all that it means to keep a good conversation going served him as another suitably complex and flexible model for knowing and learning. To this matter of the ethical and philosophical aspects of conversation I will turn in the next chapter.

So, then, just as Johnson was satisfied with neither the Cartesian nor the Lockean formula for relating thinking to being, so he also refused to subscribe to any simple causal logic to underwrite the moral, social, and philosophical teaching of the *Rambler*. As thinking and being are complexly interwoven, so, too, are literature and life. Reading an essay does not cause people to have ideas; neither do ideas cause people to behave in certain ways. Whatever shape the process may take, it is never simply linear. Indeed, as he suggests repeatedly throughout the series, whenever we do identify a simple pattern of cause and effect, we should suspect an error on our part motivated either by the urge for simplicity or by the need for self-justification.

The serial appearance of the *Rambler* and the relative brevity of the essays defer both to the comprehensive notions of life (and death) that organize and direct them and also to the generic lives that are the subject of many of the essays. This deference is grounded in what is perhaps the crucial insight and assumption of Johnson's thinking about literature and about writing in general, which he borrows from Sir Francis Bacon: "Books do not teach the use of books." He embraces and turns into one of the supports of literature precisely this seeming liability. Books, in order to come into their full power, must be engaged in a conversation with the phenomena outside of themselves collectively called *life*, similar to the kind of mutual reliance that Virginia Woolf says characterizes a healthy existence. We all have a blind spot, she observes, the size of a shilling, at the back of our heads. On account of this incorrigible blind spot, we find it paradoxically necessary to rely on one another in order to see accurately for ourselves. The inability of books to teach their own use argues a similar need for conversation between books and life. As a precondition for their creation, books must assume their own importance and independent usefulness. But this assumption which, in turn, becomes an invisible part of their structure, must never be taken for granted if those books are to serve us accurately.

In the same manner that we can use a dictionary to learn the meaning of words only when we are already acquainted with the language, so we can read literature only when are already acquainted with the life to which it belongs. Neither a dictionary nor literature can cause us to know, though both can help us to see. As no dictionary can fully define or explain a language, so no literature of a culture can fully define or explain the life of that culture. A dictionary, like literature, cannot teach its own use, nor is the use of either self-evident. A dictionary functions in relation to language as literature functions in relation to life. And like the conversational movement back and forth between using a language and using a dictionary, each movement educating us how better to use the other, so the movement back and forth between literature and life occurs in similarly conversational ways.

Shaping Johnson's sense of the necessity of this kind of conversational exchange are his notions about the ways people do and do not learn. Teachers cannot, for instance, transplant their mental models into the minds of students. Students learn by getting a faint hunch, losing it, getting it again, testing it, losing it again, many times over until finally the new idea becomes part of their model of the way things are and thus constitutive of their attitude toward the world and their resulting behavior. From that moment on, the formerly real issues of unfamiliarity and the difficulty we formerly had trying to keep the new idea in our heads no longer exist. It is impossible to forget something once it has been integrated into our knowledge and hence has become part of us. Johnson's revision of the epistemology of classical empiricism centers on this invention of a dramatic theory of knowledge in relation to persons in order to give that theory a locus in the past, present, and future of historical agents, namely ourselves. For these reasons, among others, he believed that the things we learn best are the things we learn for our own reasons, chiefly to satisfy our curiosity.[17]

Curiosity, an impulse motivating many of the plots of the *Rambler* essays, is the origin of all substantial and successful efforts toward new knowledge. Long before the practical use of any discovery is imagined there occur glimmers of pure interest, "the first start of a question." Then "desires take wing by instantaneous im-

---

17. John Holt's *How Children Learn* is an important study of this concept.

pulse" (YJ 4:186). Taking precedence over merely practical interests, the healthy excess of curiosity is a primary urge that Johnson identifies as the type of all thinking. Hence, once again, the grounds of our likeness to Don Quixote, the embodiment of such excess. The impulse toward learning is an impulse toward pleasure. Before we know what we ought to do or what would be good for us, we know what we want to find out:

> For who can believe that they who first watched the course of the stars, foresaw the use of their discoveries to the facilitation of commerce, or the mensuration of time? They were delighted with the splendor of the nocturnal skies, they found that the lights changed their places; what they admired they were anxious to understand, and in time traced their revolutions. (YJ 4:186)

Such are the primary operations of the pleasures of curiosity.

The preceding chapter examined the principle of pleasure as it inspires curiosity and supports honesty. As noted there, Johnson insists that any critic who would try to undermine the reader's pleasure in Shakespeare's plays tells a lie against the collective truth of the history of his readers' pleasure. So, too, the search for accurate pleasure, taking the form of honest curiosity, moves us instinctively to know and to understand what Isobel Grundy has characterized as "the moral and psychological relationships of one human being with another, and of the conscious, choosing self to the recalcitrant material of inclination and circumstance."[18]

THE TRUTH OF THE *RAMBLER*

More than any other of his works, this series defines a distinctive notion of the species of truth available to human beings through the kind of imaginative inquiry embodied in literature. Fredric V. Bogel has described this Johnsonian notion as asserting that literature embodies a kind of knowledge "besides the metaphysical." Referred to as "general nature," this truth, Bogel continues, "is not a metaphysical entity." Rather, it is an "'empirical' concept, of sorts, derived from the testimony of human history, the evidence of literature, and other cultural witnesses." It does not exist "anterior to the particulars" of such evidence but rather as "a wholeness, 'a quality of organized specificity and integrated detail', that arises

---

18. "Samuel Johnson: Man of Maxims?" 16.

from those particulars."[19] Bogel's comments could be taken one step further by saying that truth exists only in the present conversation. It is not merely reflected in the conversation but imagined by it. Such imagining is a complex activity because the past often exists for us as something fixed and finished. It carries, or we choose to attribute to it, an air of fatality. Reasoning backward from effects tempts one to think of causes as prior to effects. In fact they are posterior. Hence another of Johnson's reasons for calling into question unthinking adherence to conventional notions of cause and effect. Hence, too, the logic of his belief that the attempt to imagine a time before our own is an act of the imagination analogous to the creative process itself. Such thinking, as I will argue in the final chapter of this study, is quintessentially biographical.

In *Rambler* 106 Johnson identifies the dangers of failing to imagine the past. Once any tenet is generally adopted as an incontrovertible principle and has thus become a habit of thought, taken for granted, it often becomes invisible. Books in which a doctrine was first delivered are rarely examined. Even a motive as strong as curiosity is typically repressed by unthinking habit so that "we seldom look back to the arguments upon which it [what is now accepted as a principle] was first established, or can bear that tediousness of deduction, and multiplicity of evidence, by which its author was forced to reconcile it to prejudice, and fortify it in the weakness of novelty against obstinacy and envy" (YJ 4:203). Robert Boyle's importance as a scientist is unquestionable. Yet, or perhaps by virtue of this fact, "those who now adopt or enlarge his theory, very few have read the detail of his experiments. His name is, indeed, reverenced; but his works are neglected" (YJ 4:203). Through such failures on our part the past becomes unreal. When the past is made real by reading the details of Boyle's experiments and attempting to imagine their innovations, our imaginations work in ways that are as essential to inventing the future as to constructing the past.[20]

Just as teachers cannot simply transplant mental models in the form of explanations into their students' heads, neither can one generation simply absorb or graft onto their imaginations the ideas of its predecessors. Both activities require imaginative projection and identification. Johnson develops the implications of these in-

19. "The Rhetoric of Substantiality: Johnson and the Later Eighteenth Century," 472, 471.

20. On Johnson's emphasis on the importance of such reconstructive curiosity see William R. Keast, "Johnson and Intellectual History."

sights into the imaginative condition of time and history as they bear upon our relations with one another. *Rambler* 70 argues that, as our behavior may encourage and teach good behavior or discourage and warn against bad, we are thereby entrusted with both our own and one another's conduct. So, too, he argues in another of the essays, when we design a plan for "the improvement and security of mankind," by contrast with a plan designed merely for our own satisfaction, we have no merely personal right to delay that undertaking. Such responsibility is not a metaphysical truth but a palpable fact of life constituted by social circumstances, functioning in turn as a kind of safety net, protecting us against the full penalty of our individual failures. We are collectively of more potential use to one another's education than the sum total of our individual acts could ever predict or even retrospectively account for. Improbability is at the heart of learning. Education, logically speaking, should never happen.

Such necessary and seemingly natural movements from self as private entity to self as social being are, so he admits in *Rambler 99*, difficult because, as he argues more than once, "it is better to suffer wrong than to do it, and happier to be sometimes cheated than not to trust" (YJ 4:55). These comparative benefits, however, presuppose betrayal. Thus we take real chances in being part of a collective. But the complexity does not end here. In the same essay Johnson introduces another related matter: "The necessities of our condition require a thousand offices of tenderness, which mere regard for the species will never dictate" (YJ 4:166). Benevolence, fellow feeling, and acts on behalf of others are not the result of a minimalist ethic, a lowest common denominator, or even a parts-to-whole kind of thinking. As Chapter 4 will examine in *Rasselas*, the healthy instinct to take risks in helping others and to take the chance of being sometimes cheated are both inescapable aspects of the drama of education synonymous with life itself.

In his essay "Towards an Understanding of Johnson's *Rambler*," Patrick O'Flaherty discusses what he calls two "able" but "limited" approaches to these essays. One is Paul Fussell's emphasis on Johnson's habit of "tossing off these important essays in an effort to meet press deadlines." The other is the argument of Leopold J. Damrosch, Jr., that "Johnson strategically contrived reversals and conceived alternatives in order to force readers to think for themselves, to jar them towards the truth." Both approaches, O'Flaherty argues, mistakenly emphasize method or mode in individual essays and give "insufficient attention to what Johnson's overriding purpose throughout the *Rambler* actually is," namely as he states it himself in the final essay: "to inculcate wisdom or piety." O'Flaherty argues that "when Johnson thought he knew the truth, he told the truth as directly as he could." He continues, "It is not the circumstances or method of composition that determines the final shape of a *Rambler* essay as much as the difficulties inherent in a given subject and Johnson's determination not to oversimplify it. . . . [and his interest] in improving the lot of men and advancing civilization."[21] Telling the truth as best he knew it and refusing to oversimplify the inherent difficulties of his subject matter were two of Johnson's principal aims as a writer. These aims, in turn, join with his belief that time is the "prime condition governing human life,"[22] as well as with his model of conversation as a figure for our responsibility to imagine other people as real. Considered in the context of writing, this responsibility chiefly takes the form of two warnings. We should never assume, on the one hand, that others will necessarily be interested in what interests us; nor that, on the other, they cannot follow us in our farthest flights of mind.

It is thus not surprising that Johnson was especially sensitive to the twin errors of pedantry and condescension, which he examines specifically in *Rambler* 173, but whose significance applies throughout the series. Pedantry and condescension are errors not limited to writers and scholars alone. They are much more pervasive because each is an error in thinking about other people, specifically an error in logical typing, which is to say an error in organizing and classifying knowledge. Because they are fundamentally related, each arising from the same mistaken conception, they typically occur in alternation, one serving as the false corrective to the other. Pedantry and condescension alike mistakenly value power over truth and management over both truth and acquaintance.

Errors, so Johnson often observes, are easier to define than right behavior, although the latter is instantly recognizable by virtue of its distinct organization. *Rambler* 99, considered earlier, describes the general principle informing this important perception, as it intersects specifically with how we perceive our mutual obligations as human beings: "The necessities of our condition require a thousand offices of tenderness, which mere regard for the species will

21. "Towards an Understanding," 524, 527, 534.
22. From Geoffrey Tillotson, "Time in *Rasselas*," 97.

never dictate" (YJ 4:166). Here Johnson identifies the necessity of a kind of imaginative excess directing our behavior toward one another. Though it cannot be rationally specified or measured, it is no less necessary and real for being impressionistic. This phenomenological aspect of ethics, so Johnson believed, must be admitted and reckoned with.

Cumulatively the series acquaints the reader with this imprecisely specifiable but indispensable kind of behavior. The same unnamed and even unsought but successfully discerned object is identified by the travelers in *Rasselas*. For Johnson the necessity of the belief in things invisible is not restricted to religion. Nor are the delicate intuitions directing us to supply "a thousand offices of tenderness" anything less than crucial equipment for living. They provide a context and a medium for human relations while their absence leaves us feeling estranged. As good health generally goes unnoticed until interrupted by illness, so the operations of these invisible and inexpressible directives are noticed more often by their absence or suspension than by their habitual operations.

Just as good health is not properly conceived of or discerned as simply the opposite of illness, neither should goodness be seen to function in simple opposition to its seeming opposite, evil. Symmetrical thinking is rarely applicable to human activities, and in this realm logical typing is usually a serious error. Even when it is not a logical error, it is a strategic one since simple opposites, because they are grounded in similar thinking, perpetuate rather than correct errors.[23] Being at direct odds with one another, they do not have the conceptual or imaginative leverage necessary to revise one another. Genuine correction and revision are distinguished by the way they offer more than symmetrical and hence escalating opposition. These insights are distinctly un-Cartesian in the way they refuse to take as their first principle the ideal of self-control and by implication the aim of managing others. In the *Rambler* these aims give way to the ideal of maintaining a successful conversation, an aim that redefines the conventional measures of satisfaction and accomplishment in terms that no longer originate from an assumed binary opposition of self and other.

While Addison and Steele in their two earlier series dramatized

23. For a discussion of symmetrical, which is to say antagonistic, thinking see Gregory Bateson's "The Cybernetics of 'Self': A Theory of Alcoholism" in *Steps to an Ecology of Mind*, 309–37.

how the individual becomes socialized in matters of religion, knowledge, and manners, Johnson dramatizes the limits of human control in directing what happens in our encounters with other people. With the ideal of management displaced, the individual is given more responsibility, if less power in the conventional sense of the word. Conversation serves for him as a figure depicting the network of interrelations in which biographical thinking occurs. This is the social expression of his phenomenology of mind. The drama of conversation, its pleasures and advantages, its dangers and liabilities, is a metonymy for the interdependence that defines the condition of our learning and our living.

The true force and implications of the exhortation in *Rambler* 70, cited earlier, can now be thoroughly appreciated: "Every one should consider himself as entrusted, not only with his own conduct, but with that of others; and as accountable, not only for the duties which he neglects, or the crimes that he commits, but for that negligence and irregularity which he may encourage or inculcate" (YJ 4:6). Although this insight into the condition of our interrelatedness and mutual responsibility is not original, his depiction of this condition that characterizes our earthly lives is distinctively his own in its simplicity and in the force with which it earns assent. This insight is also the origin of his compelling interest in biography and his conception of biography as neither simply form nor subject matter but as a way of ordering and understanding experience.

In his advice, "It is better sometimes to be cheated than not to trust," lies the key to Johnson's vision of what is at stake in the condition of our interrelatedness and the prospect that knowledge is a subjective activity whereby one becomes briefly or enduringly committed to living out and out of new ideas.[24] He identified this condition as synonymous with learning itself and with the fact of its being not simply an activity but an essential quality of existence. Knowing and learning were for him synonymous with one another and with life. In the way we become personally committed to what we learn lies the distinctive character of human learning as personal knowledge. The changes we undergo in order to learn are a personal commitment. We invest nothing less than our identity in

24. Bateson discusses the ways human beings are committed to their knowledge in "The Group Dynamics of Schizophrenia," in *Steps to an Ecology of Mind*, 228–43.

learning and in order to learn. Hence the reason for our vulnerability and our disappointment either when learning goes wrong or
when what we have learned is called into question. When learning
is at stake, it is we ourselves who are profoundly at risk. Education
gone wrong inevitably brings pain and confusion. Yet to avoid these
risks would be to tamper with the grounds of our identity and to
risk the dissolution of self.

In the final *Rambler* essay Johnson takes leave of the reader by
invoking time, less as the reason for or cause of his decision to end
the series than as its context, just as it has been the context of all
the preceding work: "Time, which puts an end to all human pleasures and sorrows, has likewise concluded the labours of the
Rambler" (YJ 5:315). The distinction made here between cause and
context is significant as it bears upon the author's vision of how we
learn, not in a manner that can be charted causally, but rather in a
way that is best pictured as a drama of relations, situations, and
circumstances. Our contemporary, Gregory Bateson, is Johnsonian
in his conviction that we can genuinely learn only what is made
available to us by the circumstances of living and the experience of
successfully communicating with those around us. There is always
a pattern to our learning. It is impossible to learn at random. But
the forms and rhythms of our learning are as various as life itself.
And this perception on Johnson's part helps explain his interest in
and focus on conversation and its vagaries as a model for learning.
Like the anecdote of his kicking the stone until he rebounded from
it in order to refute Berkeley's idealism, the drama of conversation
is an instance of how he understood the conventional notions of
cause and effect to be inadequate to describe and account for the
way things happen and the way we think. The *Rambler* inhabits
less the Newtonian world, where objects are real and fundamentally constitutive of a larger reality, than it does his own distinctive
rendering of the Berkeleyan world of context and communication
where messages are the real thing.

Johnson does not, of course, entirely overlook the usefulness of
the Newtonian model of reality because his assertions never rely
upon radical negations. There is, to be sure, subject matter in his
world, and it is significant. In his final essay, looking back over the
two-year history of the *Rambler*, he lists the kinds of essays he has
written: the excursions of fancy, the disquisitions of criticism, the
pictures of life, and the essays professedly serious. But these cate-

gories of subject matter, real though they may be, are located within the context of time. From the perspective of this context they are cast in relation to one another in a manner that invites us to entertain alternative assumptions to those of certainty and power that underwrite the construction of conventional categories of knowledge.

This deconstruction places the reader once again in the realm of personal knowledge, attention now alerted to the way this notion necessarily extends out into a system ranging well beyond the limits of the mind or of self narrowly conceived. As for instance, to borrow again from Bateson, when one is cutting down a tree: "Each stroke of the axe is modified or corrected, according to the shape of the cut face of the tree left by the previous stroke. This self-corrective (i.e., mental) process is brought about by a total system, tree-eyes-brain-muscles-axe-stroke-tree; and it is this total system that has the characteristics of immanent mind."[25] A similar image of mind immanent in the acts it performs is carried by the *Rambler*'s emphasis on our condition of interrelatedness. Whether positively or negatively, our lives participate in a network of relations. In this network the success and failure of communication are always the issues principally at stake. It is this condition of our being, the fact of our involvement in a system far larger than the self, with which the Rambler concludes the series.

Johnson never denied that human beings' relations with one another are often discouraging and destructive: "We are by our occupations, education and habits of life divided almost into different species, which regard one another for the most part with scorn and malignity" (YJ 5:88). But whether for good or ill, we are always implicated in one another's lives—by positive affection, by alienating suspicion, or by the sense of our common obligation to contribute, as we can, to the whole. While such an observation may be a commonplace, Johnson makes it resonate with the force of genuine repetition.

As we are related to one another constructively and destructively, positively and negatively, through love and hate, praise and blame, we take from these attitudes one of our principal orientations toward life. Yet however complex such a view may be, it is an inadequate perspective without the complementary viewpoint expressed in *Rambler* 127:

25. "The Cybernetics of 'Self,' " in ibid., 317.

> He that never extends his view beyond the praises or rewards of men, will be dejected by neglect and envy, or infatuated by honours and applause. But the consideration that life is only deposited in his hands to be employed in obedience to a Master who will regard his endeavours, not his success, would have preserved him from trivial elations and discouragements, and enabled him to proceed with constancy and chearfulness, neither enervated by commendation, nor intimidated by censure. (YJ 4:315)

While not denying the importance of praise and rewards, honors and applause, and their opposites, Johnson here imagines a space of thinking entirely different, one that neither duplicates nor offers a simple alternative to such binary categories as hope and fear. Like his view of the complementary pairs, objectivity and subjectivity, reason and imagination, cause and context, the two perspectives identified in this passage do not merely fulfill one another; they make one another real, both serving to imagine what the other cannot.[26] At the point where each leaves off, where each cannot within the terms of its system do what the other is equipped to do, the other picks up and carries on.

The Vanity of Human Wishes (1749) offers a useful retrospective on this chapter's discussion of the *Rambler.* Like *The Vision of Theodore* and the Preface to *The Preceptor,* this poem, which enacts two fundamentally different ways of understanding, is a metaphor of Johnson's mind. One of these ways is observation. Empirically based, symmetrical, and emulative, observation directs the first 342 lines of the poem, giving us a view of the world from its characteristic orientation, empowering us to see in certain habitual ways and thereby not to see in others. Observation is a habit of symmetrical thinking that organizes the world into pairs of opposites: like and unlike, successful and unsuccessful, worthy and unworthy, to name only a few. This kind of thinking functions characteristically by gathering evidence, constructing categories to organize that evidence, comparing and contrasting, judging and assessing, gathering more evidence, and so forth. There is no logical reason for such thinking ever to come to an end of its own accord. Like the travelers in *Rasselas* who search for the happy choice of life, there is no reason internal to the search itself to end it. The momentum of their pursuit has an internal self-propelling logic. Only by the intersection of another epistemology, introduc-

---

26. In *Samuel Johnson* Bate discusses what he calls "the dialectic and bisociative character of Johnson's mind" (534).

ing terms that this system cannot imagine, are the travelers empowered to redirect their drama by reimagining it.

In *The Vanity of Human Wishes* this redirection is introduced by the familiar question:

> Where then shall Hope and Fear their objects find?
> Must dull Suspence corrupt the stagnant mind?
> Must helpless man, in ignorance sedate,
> Roll darkling down the torrent of his fate?
>
> (YJ 6:107–8)

From the perspective not only of all the evidence but also of the poem's manner of proceeding up to this point, the implied answer would seem to be an obvious and foregone conclusion. But for Johnson this rhetorical question with its air of fatality alerts us to the need for another kind of thinking and a different manner of seeing in order to renovate the poem's logic. And so the poem concludes in a prayer for the ability to pray. Dematerializing its subject matter by introducing a meta-communicative level, the poem imports into itself a new consciousness. This new consciousness makes visible retrospectively the poem's methodology of observation and its underlying materialist assumptions. In order to become real and truly useful such assumptions must function in relation to another imaginative possibility, as here, the perspective of prayer grounded in a different epistemology. The assumptions of this epistemology are not symmetrical and power-based, but complementary and participatory.

For Johnson the spectacle of discovery, of revising our thinking, of coming to see old things in a new way, was always remarkable because it is never predicated in or anticipated by what comes before. Any discovery, "while it was yet unknown, was believed impossible" (YJ 4:325). Our current point of view always seems natural, necessary, and certain. It thus generally fills the imagination completely, preempting other possibilities. Hence the importance for healthy, creative thinking of considering those who in the drama of history were "more daring than the rest, adventured to bid defiance to prejudice and censure" (YJ 4:325) and who made discoveries of what was thought to be impossible. Hence, too, the most important use of history, the subject of the second half of this study. History, like biography, is less accurately conceived of as a kind of subject matter than as a kind of thinking in which we exercise our imaginations in the creative process. Whether it be reviewing a passage from Martial in the form of a *Rambler* epigraph or recovering details of Boyle's experiments, such acts of the imagination are the movements of a healthy mind, earning its inheritance from the past and inventing a life in the present. This way of thinking through the past in relation to the present and future demonstrates once again the importance of combining invention with revision in order to create genuine repetition.

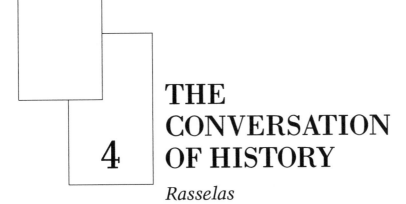

THE
CONVERSATION
OF HISTORY

4

Rasselas

WHEN DRAMA IS NOT A PLAY

It is time to think now once again about Johnson at Edial in 1736, trying one last time to become a teacher while also beginning to write his tragedy *Irene*. These two activities were in part a yoking of opposites: the humble with the high, the dogged with the aspiring, the locally earnest with the outward bound. And yet they had their similarities, as well. The creative cause of each was Johnson's earnestness, their immediate outcome, failure. Both laid the groundwork for later successes that no one, perhaps especially their author, could have foreseen.

He seems to have learned from his experiments with teaching and with playwriting something about what Kenneth Burke calls "the factor of interest in the business of communication":

> Even if one speaks very clearly and simply on a subject of great moment to himself, for instance, one is hardly communicating in the desired sense if his auditor does not care in the least what he is saying. . . . We interest a man by dealing with his interests. . . . The mere fact that something is to a man's interests is no guaranty that he will be interested in it. It is tremendously to people's interests that they should understand the causes of war—but it is very hard to get them interested in the subject.[1]

Authors should not assume their readers' interests to be identical with their own. Nor should they assume that their readers will invariably be interested in what is to their own best advantage. But Johnson was in his twenties when he began writing *Irene* and did not yet understand this fact about human nature, nor had he yet inferred its implications for writing. More likely than not, he still

---

1. *Permanence and Change: An Anatomy of Purpose*, 37, 38.

thought it sufficient simply to tell people what he thought they needed to know.

From his later work can be measured the distance he subsequently traveled in coming to learn about the factor of interest. This insight informs such observations as "we love better to be pleased than to be taught" (LP 2:144). It inspires the subtle precision of his comment about education in *Rambler 3*: "Men must not only be persuaded of their errors, but reconciled to their guide; they must not only confess their ignorance, but, what is still less pleasing, must allow that he from whom they are to learn is more knowing than themselves" (YJ 3:15). Such observations make clear the degree to which he overcame the liability of his earnestness, transforming it into a searching sensitivity to whatever may interfere with learning. This same sensitivity combined with both a greater tolerance and a stronger determination to help us correct our all too frequent failure to take interest in what is in our best interest.

Chapter 1 of this study proposed how Johnson's teaching experiences informed and touched a readiness in him that later found more successful forms of expression. As a frame for discussing *Rasselas*, the present chapter proposes that in writing this tale he solved the problem of form that he had encountered in *Irene*. Just as, according to Boswell, Johnson was perpetually a poet, always thinking in imagery, so too he was perpetually a dramatist, or at least his thinking was structurally dramatic. For this reason, playwriting as activity and the play as formal construct were unsuitable to his imagination and skills. They too literally transcribed the essential manner of his thinking and thus undermined its power to move his ideas forcefully, strategically, and with sufficient difference. Johnson was thus correct in his early instinct for drama but wrong in deciding that drama was the form into which he should channel that instinct. What he needed to find in order to mobilize his inclination and his gifts was, to borrow once again from Burke, a *perspective by incongruity*.[2] In the extended essay form of *Rasselas* he found an appropriate expression for the failed *Irene*. This play, as Boswell remarked, "will furnish a rich store of noble sentiments, fine imagery, and beautiful language," but it fails by being "deficient in pathos, in that delicate power of touching the human

2. Burke defines the term "perspective by incongruity" in *Attitudes toward History*, 308–14, and applies it in *Permanence and Change*.

feelings, which is the principal end of the drama."[3] In his fiction, Johnson repaired this deficiency.

The extended essay was for him a strategic choice for channeling his powers and inclinations more successfully because he wrote this form as an attenuated play. Or, to put it another way, Johnson mobilized his ideas best and most naturally as agents in the world—as drama. Again Burke is helpful:

> The essayist's terms serve to organize a set of interrelated emphases, quite as Othello, Iago, and Desdemona are inter-related emphases. There are "hero" and "villain" terms, with subsidiary terms distributed about these two poles like iron filings in a magnetic field, and tracing somewhat of a "graded series" between them. Emphases cannot "contradict" one another, so far as the "total plot" is concerned, any more than Iago's function in the play can be said to contradict Othello's.[4]

Rasselas succeeds dramatically where *Irene* fails as a play because with this form Johnson could make his thoughts sufficiently mobile to show how the most useful and healthiest kind of thinking succeeds in upsetting relationships while still preserving form. He uses the conversations among the characters in this tale to dramatize, though not in play form, one of the crucial facts, as he saw it, about earthly life: "In order that we may have some guarantee of arriving at the same opinion about an idea, the minimal requirement is that we should have had different opinions about it in the first place. If two men want to agree they really have to contradict one another first. Truth is the daughter of discussion, not of sympathy."[5] In a similar way *Rasselas* communicates its ideas through dramatic conflict that upsets relationships while preserving form. This paradox is the narrative's major factor of interest. It emerges chiefly by contrast with the dramatic possibility always threatening to undermine interest, namely boredom.

BOREDOM AND ITS OPPOSITES

The travelers who escape from the happy valley in search of the happy choice of life experience many feelings during their travels—

---

3. *Life*, 1:198. In chapter 5 (*"Irene"*) of *Samuel Johnson and the Tragic Sense*, Leopold Damrosch, Jr., discusses Johnson's failure in writing this play to "draw upon the deep understanding of the tragic in human life which he was developing during this period and which found moving expression in the *Life of Savage*" (111).

4. *Attitudes toward History*, 312.

5. Bachelard, *The Philosophy of No*, 114.

terror, disappointment, pleasure, curiosity, suspicion, perplexity, grief, sympathy, and joy, among them. But markedly absent and notably so, both in the context of life in the valley and the subsequent motives for their escape, is the feeling of boredom. In this fundamental sense their journey, despite its disappointments, succeeds. The psychology of boredom, its meaning and antidotes, is central to an understanding of Johnson's distinctive approach as critic and moralist to literature and to life. Aspects of this psychology of boredom in *Rasselas*, particularly "the hunger of the imagination" never satisfied by finite earthly activity, have been richly considered by a number of Johnsonians.[6] But there is more to say on the subject in light of the tale's examination of the intersection of boredom and history.

This chapter examines how in *Rasselas* Johnson sizes up the situation of boredom and comes to see history, along with its most significant expressive form, biography, as strategic solutions to this problem. By strategic solution, I mean what Johnson meant, not a recipe or prescription for avoiding boredom but a way of identifying the problem, naming it, and by that very naming to draft the terms that, when achieved, will be recognized to constitute an adequate solution. This distinction, which Chapter 1 examined in detail, is nice but not small. By history, I have in mind neither a mere chronology nor a specialized professional undertaking but the natural interest and function of the mind "to push back the narrow confines of the fleeting present moment so that what we are doing may be judged in the light of what we have done and what we hope to do."[7]

The happy valley is an experiment in creating a society without

6. One thinks particularly of the work of Bate in *The Achievement of Samuel Johnson* and *Samuel Johnson* (notably 297–317 in the latter) and Wain in *Samuel Johnson* (particularly 209–15). This essay places itself within the critical conversation among most notably these Johnsonians: Mary Lascelles, "*Rasselas* Reconsidered"; Tillotson, "Time in *Rasselas*"; William K. Wimsatt, Jr., "In Praise of *Rasselas*: Four Notes (Converging)"; McIntosh, *The Choice of Life*; Patrick O'Flaherty, "Dr. Johnson as Equivocator: The Meaning of *Rasselas*"; Gloria Sybil Gross, "Sanity, Madness, and the Family in Samuel Johnson's *Rasselas*"; Edward Tomarken, "Travels into the Unknown: *Rasselas* and *A Journey to the Western Islands of Scotland*"; and John A. Vance, *Samuel Johnson and the Sense of History*, particularly the discussion of the kind of participatory thinking that good historical writing requires of the reader (112–17). Max Byrd comments that "a deadly serious boredom calls into question the real significance of our experience" ("Johnson's Spiritual Anxiety," 376). Lynch's *Images of Faith* discusses the moral, aesthetic, and psychological failings of boredom. Lynch characterizes boredom as a failure to embody thought and to comprehend irony.

7. Carl Becker, "Everyman his own Historian," 227.

history. Its protective and imprisoning geography, its schedule of constant delights, and the ideal pleasures built into its very architecture embody a scheme of felicity that attempts rationally to overturn the human fate of chronic dissatisfaction. The mathematical model underwriting this experiment is: the more pleasures, the more happiness. So few of the hours of life are filled with objects adequate to our imaginations and so frequently do we lack sufficient present pleasure or employment that we habitually refer to past and future for supplemental satisfactions in order to relieve the vacuities of our being.

Such a condition would seem to be a serious liability. But Johnson was astute in recognizing, as has been earlier noted, that one of the measures of good sense and a healthy mind is the capacity to convert liabilities into assets. *Rasselas* is a study of the principle informing such revisions. Life in the happy valley seems to provide an adequate sequence of present pleasures and thus to leave no such imaginative vacuities. This experiment in living without history aims to relieve the inhabitants of their constant craving and dissatisfaction with their condition as creatures in and of time. This condition, as life in the valley demonstrates, is often mistaken for longings that can be literally or even figuratively satisfied. For none of the inhabitants, however, does this additive approach to achieving happiness succeed. Most of them, as Imlac observes, are wretched. Furthermore, it is particularly disturbing to think of this place as an antechamber to the throne for young "Abissinian" royalty who await their call to service here in a place where history is programmatically excluded and hence a place which legislates against the possibility of a book entitled *The History of Rasselas, Prince of Abissinia*. Again Imlac cannily assesses the dangerous implications of this prohibition: "If we act only for ourselves, to neglect the study of history is not prudent: if we are entrusted with the care of others, it is not just" (YJ 16:112–13). The ethos of this place could only produce inadequate rulers deprived of the important qualification of knowing history and thinking historically.

Rasselas's home, then, is a prison of pleasure. It attempts to minimize the fear of life and death by simulating an eternal present. But this attempt results in the inhabitants being treated like the daughters of the families in Cairo whom Nekayah subsequently interviews. She discovers that "their grief, however, like their joy, was transient; every thing floated in their mind unconnected with the past or future" (YJ 16:92). Such an attempt offers quite obvious attractions. Its distinctive logic that reduces the uncertainty of history has a definite, if specious, appeal. Significantly lacking is the cooperative competition essential to healthy, as opposed to totalitarian, politics for which the model is good conversation.[8] Thus it is surely no accident that Rasselas yearns for good conversation in the happy valley. This yearning is a glimmer of good health amid his several other symptoms of unhealthiness—his boredom, selfishness, and indecision.

Johnson examines the common fear of agonistic development and offers solutions that involve the use of history in its public and private forms. His answer first and foremost is that by recognizing how much is to be lost by reducing the uncertainty and fearfulness of conversation, one comes to see the right course of action. By refusing to participate in history and conversation, one encounters the unanswerable opponent of a resolutely mute and thereby dangerous world. By accepting participation one begins to talk with the world. If this attempt is not always successful, it is nonetheless crucial to have made it. The process is, in no small part, its own legitimate end.

The implications of these insights are no less serious for the education of a prince than for the development of an ordinary person. They are also essential to political freedom. Paradoxically, insofar as the totalitarian state attempts to eradicate history and historical thinking, that state cannot generate a description adequate to the real circumstances it aims to encompass. Hence by silencing the opponent and thus denying the possibility of that mature collective revelation to which disagreement is essential, totalitarian politics ultimately dooms itself. When Rasselas decides to leave home, he enters into the many-voiced drama of history described by Burke as if to gloss *Rasselas*. In answer to the question, where does the drama of history get its materials, Burke replies:

> From the "unending conversation" that is going on at the point in history when we are born. Imagine that you enter a parlor. You come late. When you arrive, others have long preceded you, and they are engaged in a heated discussion, a discussion too heated for them to pause and tell you exactly what it is about. In fact, the discussion had already

8. For a discussion of conversation as a model for philosophy, see particularly Richard A. Rorty's *Philosophy and the Mirror of Nature*, particularly chapter 8, section 5, "Philosophy in the Conversation of Mankind"; and Kenneth Burke's "The Philosophy of Literary Form" in *The Philosophy of Literary Form: Studies in Symbolic Action*, 107–12.

begun long before any of them got there, so that no one present is qualified to retrace for you all the steps that had gone before. You listen for a while, until you decide that you have caught the tenor of the argument; then you put in your oar. Someone answers; you answer him; another comes to your defense; another aligns himself against you, to either the embarrassment or gratification of your opponent, depending upon the quality of your ally's assistance. However, the discussion is interminable. The hour grows late, you must depart. And you do depart, with the discussion still vigorously in progress.[9]

This conception of history is denied by the happy valley where the royal palace itself, symbolic of the local ethos, "was built as if suspicion herself had dictated the plan," the inhabitants imprisoned by an iron gate and confined to the eternal present by the valley's schedule of speciously delightful but essentially repressive and infantilizing activities. There is pleasure, to be sure. But pleasure occurring solely in the present is totalitarianism because it denies the imagination's freedom to conceive of itself as other than it is in the present moment. Johnson anticipates analyses of the modern totalitarian state by perceiving the dangers of excluding history, an exclusion that tyrannizes over the mind by denying one of its most significant, healthy, and subversive functions of thinking historically. To think historically is always subversive because it leads one to question, debate, and contradict.

Johnson's lifelong commitment to these activities is exemplified in the account of his conversation with a friend during his last illness:

> The friend cautiously mentioned a certain lack of Christian charity, especially apparent when Johnson contradicted people in conversation. "Now what harm," asked the slightly ruffled Johnson, turning to Boswell, "does it do to any man to be contradicted?" Boswell suggested that the rough manner had hurt some weak-nerved people. "And who is the worse for that?" thundered the ailing man, adding: "I know no such weak-nerved people."[10]

It would be mistaken to read this anecdote simply as evidence of Johnson's egotism or of his habit of talking for victory, although some of each may be present. The concluding statement is one of his typical renderings of moral exhortation in the form of simple

9. *Philosophy of Literary Form*, 110–11.
10. Cited (n.p. given in Boswell's *Life*) in Manfred Weidhorn, "The Conversation of Common Sense," 3.

description, as Paul K. Alkon has identified this technique.[11] Hyperbole is surely intended, at least in part, to communicate a descriptive truth about the necessity of healthy debate. To be too weak-nerved to engage in contradiction has, from Johnson's point of view, implications far too dangerous to risk.

If all the inhabitants of the happy valley experience "vacancies of attention" and suffer "the tediousness of time," only a very few are curious enough to inquire after the reason a place rationally calculated to give pleasure does not always please. If they inquired, they would discover the distinction between the specious and merely placating repetition of pleasure that obliterates time, on the one hand, and the genuine repetition of pleasure that depends on and emphasizes time, on the other. The former fails because it is mere redundancy; the latter, which the travelers in *Rasselas* regularly enjoy, succeeds because it affirms what Martin Heidegger has called "the connectedness of life."[12] This connectedness serves, in turn, as the basis of historical thinking, which values genuine repetition. Genuine repetition, which is never boring, is in turn grounded in a healthy attitude toward similarity and difference. Carl Becker's adage, "every man his own historian," identifies Johnson's sense of the centrality of history, understood to be a mode of thought, to practical daily life. It is a necessity, not an occasional or specialized discipline, and it functions like acquaintance.[13]

ACQUAINTANCE AND HISTORY

Rasselas is not a narrative of character in the usual sense of that term. But it is a tale about human acquaintance, about how people understand one another, about what familiarity with another person means and what it involves, and about the relation of these activities to education. Furthermore, this fiction considers how the activity of acquaintance, so important in education, also serves as a model for historical thinking. Biography is the dramatic form taken by such acts of acquaintance, as people tell and listen to their

11. *Samuel Johnson and Moral Discipline*, xi–xii.
12. Joel Weinsheimer in his notable essay, "Writing about Literature and through It," uses this Heideggerian notion as the basis for distinguishing specious from genuine repetition in criticism. Genuine repetition, Weinsheimer argues, values the unity of discontinuity that makes possible relation to rather than identity with history.
13. James Noxon makes this argument in "Human Nature: General Theory and Individual Lives."

own and other people's lives. Like the drama of education, central to the plot of *Rasselas*, the drama of successful acquaintance occurs in unpredictable, though not incomprehensible, ways through time. These ways are fundamentally biographical. The activity of acquaintance as a model for understanding proceeds by the imaginative procedures of projection and identification. It contrasts with the method of science that values explanation as its aim and proceeds by causal analysis. Defined early in *Rasselas* as the primary strategy for sizing up a situation, acquaintance proceeds by concurrently deemphasizing subject matter and emphasizing the importance of accurate and safe communication.

This emphasis is predicted in the opening sentence that, by its inconclusiveness, invites varying interpretations over time: "Ye who listen with credulity to the whispers of fancy, and pursue with eagerness the phantoms of hope; who expect that age will perform the promises of youth, and that the deficiencies of the present day will be supplied by the morrow; attend to the history of Rasselas prince of Abissinia" (YJ 16:7). One might say that the story's conclusion is implicit in this syntax and that to express the final meaning one need only insert negatives into each of the parallel phrases. But *Rasselas* offers more possibilities for genuine repetition than any single reading of this passage could admit. And it seems appropriate for a narrative that ends without simple closure also to begin this way. Furthermore, since there exist in the tale other words of advice that unquestionably require explicit interpretations (the maid's comment about the broken cup: "What cannot be repaired is not to be regretted"; and Imlac's observation on choices, that "one cannot drink at once from the mouth and source of the Nile"), the variety of interpretative possibilities of the opening advice either by the same or by different readers over time is underscored.

Implicit in the diction and tone of the opening is an authorial stance that withholds itself from telling the reader what to think, for to do so would deny the possibility of returning to the story over time. The travelers' search in *Rasselas* is indeed a search for an alternative to the unpleasing captivity of false repetition characterizing life in the happy valley. The search for a livable version of such captivity in the form of genuine repetition is not wrong if it is neither literalized nor used to control other people's minds and imaginations but rather pursued with healthy flexibility. This opening movement toward identifying healthy and interesting repetition continues when Rasselas meets his former teacher. Concerned and perplexed by the prince's refusal to join in the supposed general happiness of life in the valley, the old man asks him why he is unhappy. At first the prince is annoyed by the question: "Why does this man thus intrude upon me; shall I be never suffered to forget those lectures which pleased only while they were new, and to become new again must be forgotten?" (YJ 16:15). Schoolroom lectures may be of use but are rarely of interest to hear a second time. By contrast, subjects or approaches admitting of genuine repetition please and interest us time and again, their interest depending neither on forgetfulness nor on artifice. The events that follow demonstrate the repeated pleasures of true education.

Learning motivated by desire, by contrast with rote study, finds its origin in the investigator's own agenda of inquiry. Unlike the dissatisfaction of mechanical memory, learning that is personally motivated occurs from the inside out. Yet however uninteresting certain repetitions may be and however much one owes it to oneself to avoid boredom, other obligations, so Johnson dramatizes in this scene, may sometimes compete for and even override the personal responsibility to seek out meaningful, enjoyable repetition. In this instance the competing responsibility is the prince's decent sensitivity to show his former teacher respect and affection. He temporarily sets aside annoyance, patiently listening to a man who now seemingly can teach him nothing more. Such improvisatory flexibility testifies to a healthy mind that can shift agilely from its own concerns and desires to those of another. If this seems a small matter, one should remember that Johnson regularly reminds us how the presence or absence of such acts collectively over the years determines the general emotional tenor of our lives.

In the course of their conversation the teacher finds himself surprised at the prince's "new species of affliction." How can anyone be unhappy in the happy valley? Attempting to correct his former pupil's mistaken view and no doubt also wishing to make himself once again useful to the student whose reverence he once commanded, he lectures the prince on his comparative pleasures and security here in the valley. If he knew the dangers and afflictions of the world, his teacher remarks confidently, he would appreciate his life in the valley. In a manner he could not have predicted, the teacher's comments help his former student define his discontent: "I have already enjoyed too much, give me something to desire." This discovery is the first in a series that demonstrate how insights may be motivated by surprising circumstances and how the drama of conversation is the midwife of ideas. The teacher's words, against their intention, help Rasselas define his discontent and imagine a cure.

The scene is an intricate comedy. While no one fails completely, success is difficult to define because it requires a keen eye for revising expectations and for seeing useful information where none was expected. A new economy of education has emerged out of unpromising circumstances. Rasselas's teacher has made himself once again useful to his student, though not in the way he had hoped. And to the prince's surprise, his teacher has given him a new lesson. Thus what began as an unwanted intrusion has become for the prince a happy accident. Furthermore, the contrast between the teacher's intended meaning and his student's interpretation illustrates a simple but important fact about education, namely that it occurs between people in a particular set of circumstances wherein more meaning can be generated than any single participant could ever anticipate or even, after the fact, fully account for.

Rasselas has not altered the literal meaning of his teacher's remarks. But he has revised their implications for practical action, and this transformation makes all the difference. The intention and reception of a speaker's words are not always identical, their effects not always calculable in simple ways. They fall upon the ears of others who have their own histories of experience and expectation and thus hear the same words differently. These autobiographical and biographical aspects of conversation, education, and history interested Johnson for their potential to be either liabilities or assets in the drama of education, in particular, and of creativity, in general. In writing *Rasselas* he composed a story to dramatize these interrelated issues.

My intention in making the foregoing claims is not to transform Johnson into a relativist. He did not believe communication to be subject to infinite and infinitely acceptable interpretations. But he did believe that communication is both difficult and promising in ways that no merely rational schema can fully account for. Rather than being amazed at misunderstanding, Johnson, like Bertrand Russell, as earlier noted, was amazed at our capacity to understand one another as often as we do. Our success, however, is difficult to measure and certainly cannot be measured by any single individual's standards. One person's failure may be another person's success. Both success and failure in communication must be measured collectively and cumulatively among us all over time.

Meaning, then, as it unfolds in the exchange between Rasselas and his former teacher, is made according to the various agenda of interest and expectations brought to the conversation by each participant. In the course of this conversation he unexpectedly learns once again from his teacher. But now, because the prince has established his own distinctive stance toward the meaning of the lesson, he may learn in a manner that makes genuine repetition possible. We can repeat without being merely repetitious only what is truly our own. The sum of pleasure and energy that the prince experiences after this conversation, which seemed to offer nothing pertinent to his present circumstances, comes from its meaning now connected with a decision and a plan he can begin to claim as his own.

The conclusion of this episode focuses on the old man's discontent in finding his intentions reversed by Rasselas's interpretation. But once again the frame shifts from the narrowly personal to something larger that is as significant as the comedy of accidentally successful teaching. As Rasselas moves from boredom to annoyance to thoughtfulness to curiosity and finally to hope, his teacher moves quickly from discontent to resignation. The different trajectories that characterize their respective ages illustrate how our thinking and feeling unfold distinctively over the historical continuum of our lives. The prince's circumstances have not changed. But now, thanks simply to a new thought that organizes his prospects differently, he imagines the world differently. Hope may indeed be a feeling, but it is a feeling arising from one's point of view. Thus it has a philosophical basis. As hope begins to replace boredom, Rasselas can begin to imagine his future.[14]

His hope at this stage, however, is incomplete because it is hope only for himself. As Imlac later comments, his decision to be a poet radically changed his point of view: "I saw every thing with a new purpose; my sphere of attention was suddenly magnified: no kind of knowledge was to be overlooked" (YJ 16:41–42). This kind of kaleidoscopic conversion fascinated Johnson for the evidence it gives of the mind's capacity to reconceive and reperceive reality by shifting viewpoints and by looking at the world from different angles over time. But these different angles remain incomplete until

14. A relevant discussion of the psychology of hope through an evocation of archetypal pathology appears in James Hillman's *Re-Visioning Psychology*, particularly chapter 2, "Pathologizing or Falling Apart," and chapter 4, "Dehumanizing or Soul-making."

they can be shared with and used by others, which is to say, until they become the subject of conversation and thus are of use and interest to others. It is thus appropriate that Imlac's greatest unhappiness in the happy valley comes from the melancholy recognition that his knowledge is no longer of use to anyone.

Pleased by his discovery of a possibility for happiness in seeing the world's affliction, Rasselas now considers himself to be the "master of a secret stock of happiness, which he could enjoy only by concealing it" (YJ 16:17). His response is in keeping with the condition of secrecy informing the valley's totalitarian politics, architecture, and pattern of human relations that combine to oversimplify the temporal, moral, and emotional complexity of the operations of the human imagination. At this point in the story, when the prince discovers his "secret stock of happiness," he becomes guilty of a version of the dramatic pretense shared by the other inhabitants of the valley. Melancholy and idle, they wish to spread their misery by enticing others to join them. Without revealing his own discovery, he encourages his fellow prisoners to enjoy their condition. While Rasselas's behavior is not actively malicious, his encouraging false enjoyment of the eternal present is unworthy of a future monarch. These motifs of secrecy and pretense, introduced early in the tale to exemplify the valley's dangerous politics, recur throughout the journey to come.

LYING AND ITS OPPOSITES

To consider the psychology of this web of pretenses, lies, and secrecy directs us to the heart of Johnson's thinking about the possibility of succeeding in our relations with others. Considering this matter also contributes to defining his view of the uses of history. History's significant functions are to gather truth, restore accuracy, and bring to light what is hidden. Its yet more encompassing importance lies in the way it depends for its very functioning on our actively protecting the general condition of truth and accuracy in human communication and simultaneously measures our success in so doing. As Sissela Bok argues in her study of lying, physical violence and lying are the two principal forms of human destructiveness. They are similar in that each threatens society at its most basic level of functioning. Johnson, like Bok, identifies the antisocial act of lying as a fundamental act of violence against our fellows.

Rasselas's concern with secrecy, a version of lying, is mirrored by other figures in the tale. Among these is the mechanic flyer who is designing wings to lift him above the dangers of earthly life. Fearful that his invention might fall into the wrong hands and warning the prince how dangerous this would be, he swears him to secrecy:

> If men were all virtuous, returned the artist, I should with great alacrity teach them all to fly. But what would be the security of the good, if the bad could at pleasure invade them from the sky? Against an army sailing through the clouds neither walls, nor mountains, nor seas, could afford any security. A flight of northern savages might hover in the wind, and light at once with irresistible violence upon the capital of a fruitful region that was rolling under them. (YJ 16:27–28)

The vow of secrecy proves to be comically unnecessary when the flyer's wings fail to support him and he falls into the lake. But an accidental and comic equilibrium is achieved when his wings unpredictably keep him afloat. This success recalls the earlier incident of Rasselas's conversation with his former teacher whose unwillingness to be silent led inadvertently to his becoming once again useful to his student. The intention behind the flyer's wings, like the lesson intended by the teacher, miscarries. But each turns out to have an overdetermined usefulness that could not have been predicted by any of the participants. There remains, however, the fact that both the teacher and the flyer express the distinctive ethos of the happy valley with its emphasis on isolation and its subtext of fear. The teacher expects his student to appreciate his good fortune in being imprisoned in safety and pleasure. The flyer offers him a similar isolation and protection suspended above the earth.

This repetition of episodes prepares for the entrance of Imlac, who restores the prince's imagination to healthy movement by reciting his poem on the "conditions of humanity" and telling the story of his life. In each of the prince's first two conversations the other speaker invoked fear to manipulate him—the teacher, in order to encourage him to appreciate the virtues of his current situation, and the mechanic flyer, in order to gain the prince's conspiratorial silence. But Imlac, who also mentions the fears and dangers of the world, does so in a quite different way that marks a significant new direction for the drama of education.

While the flyer and the old teacher told Rasselas stories for which they provided the interpretation, Imlac's tale makes possible true learning by allowing the listener to react independently, even to disagree. Imlac achieves this openness by combining narrative with analysis. Thus he offers the prince his first lesson in naming fearful circumstances. The remainder of the tale can be read as a search for happiness that takes the specific form of a search for ways of naming fearful and disturbing circumstances. This naming constitutes and directs the travelers' attitudes toward and strategies for dealing with the situations they encounter along their way. Here is a sample from Imlac's first vocabulary lesson, as he and Rasselas discuss some important distinctions of meaning:[15]

> "*Subordination* supposes *power* on one part and *subjection* on the other; and if power be in the hands of men, it will sometimes be abused. The vigilance of the supreme magistrate may do much, but much will still remain undone. He can never know all the crimes that are committed, and can seldom punish all that he knows."
>
> "This," said the prince, "I do not understand, but I had rather hear thee than dispute. Continue thy narration."
>
> "My father," proceeded Imlac, "originally intended that I should have no other education, than such as might qualify me for commerce; and discovering in me great strength of memory, and quickness of apprehension, often declared his hope that I should be some time the richest man in Abissinia."
>
> "Why," said the prince, "did thy father desire the increase of his wealth, when it was already greater than he durst discover or enjoy? I am unwilling to doubt thy veracity, yet inconsistencies cannot both be true."
>
> "*Inconsistencies*," answered Imlac, "cannot both be *right*, but, imputed to man, they may both be *true*. Yet *diversity* is not inconsistency. My father might expect a time of greater security. However, some desire is necessary to keep life in motion, and he, whose real wants are supplied, must admit those of fancy." (YJ 16:32–33, emphasis mine)

For the first time in the tale figures have a real conversation marked by equality and cooperation between the participants. The two speakers, one of whom has more experience than the other and thus enjoys an advantage of power, experience a wholesome measure of conversational equality. Neither participant takes advantage of the other. Neither suffers by virtue of his ignorance. The discrepancy measured here between Rasselas's untested logic and the drama of human contingency to which he is applying it serves to identify the young man's inexperience. But Johnson is less interested in exposing naïveté and inexperience than he is in exploring the service performed by the drama of conversation in bringing to

15. Knoblauch comments that "Rasselas's education is almost entirely verbal (hence, like the *Dictionary*, *Rasselas* is a text upon a text)" ("Coherence Betrayed," 250).

light the different ways different people think. If this sounds like a simple, perhaps even an overly simple observation, it is also one whose implications for identifying ourselves in history are all too often neglected.

Rasselas is indebted to Imlac for this initiation into the unending conversation of history. And it is interesting to note how this first true conversation develops. Beginning in disagreement, the discussion ends with Rasselas feeling a flicker of recognition based on his own experience. This fleeting recognition gives the prince a clue about how to enter Imlac's thinking. At the same time it makes that entry desirable. To Imlac's comment about how desires, whether real or fanciful, are necessary to keep life in motion, he gives an understated reply: "This I can in some measure conceive. I repent that I interrupted thee" (YJ 16:33). Such a connection is crucial to preserving the precondition of trust and belief necessary to an ongoing conversation of any significance.

Whereas Rasselas's meeting with his former teacher was motivated by a sense of obligation to honor the man he once reverenced and his meetings with the flyer by the lack of any better prospect, neither of these a negligible reason, his conversation with Imlac is motivated by a healthy curiosity to hear this man recite a poem about his travels. Their subsequent conversation is different from the two preceding chiefly because Imlac does not exploit his advantage of knowledge. In his first long conversation with the prince, the poet offers him a set of strategic definitions that suggest the contours of a larger chart of meanings adequate to describe actual scenes in the world. Rasselas has experience sufficient only to begin to understand a portion of Imlac's chart of meanings. But this understanding, at least for the moment, is less important than the experience of being exposed to a new way of thinking about the world. He hears new categories and is introduced to new ways of making distinctions and assessing circumstances. Such information is always as fascinating as it is empowering. Rasselas is able to learn this new way of sizing up the world precisely, if ironically, because it resembles a fictional strategy he himself had earlier attempted. After the conversation with his former teacher, the prince begins to spend his time picturing a world he has never seen. Fantasizing about coming to the rescue of an orphan virgin robbed by a faithless lover, he finds himself so powerfully moved by his own fiction (a danger identified in *Rambler* 4 nine years earlier) that he literally runs to save the young woman. Catching himself in his delusion, he proceeds to calculate sternly how much time he has wasted in mere imagining.

This pair of incidents dramatizes Johnson's notions about the stages of the mind's maturing from visionary bustle to critical mapping. These stages do not coincide simply with one's age, nor does visionary bustle completely disappear when the critical mapping establishes itself as the predominant mode. But critical mapping is requisite for adulthood and for some degree of analytical mastery of the world that, while it may not be synonymous either with complete accuracy or with success, is substantially related to our developing a sense of basic competence. Distinct yet complementary, Rasselas's fiction and Imlac's tactical vocabulary are strategies that the mind applies to understand its circumstances, to discharge its responsibilities, and to achieve its desires.

The strength of both imaginative and rational thought—thought that pictures and figures forth, and thought that analyzes and creates schema—and the quality that makes them natural allies lies in what Imlac later in the story calls the "indiscerptible power of thought." While the travelers contemplate mortality and immortality in the catacombs, their guide observes:

> "Consider your own conceptions," replied Imlac, "and the difficulty will be less. You will find substance without extension. An ideal form is no less real than material bulk: yet an ideal form has no extension. It is no less certain, when you think on a pyramid, that your mind possesses the idea of a pyramid, than that the pyramid itself is standing. . . . As is the effect such is the cause; as thought is, such is the power that thinks; a power impassive and indiscerptible." (YJ 16:173)

Johnson defines "indiscerptible" in the *Dictionary* as "not to be separated; incapable of being broken or destroyed by dissolution of parts." Thought is real and the world is real. Their joint reality, conceived and dramatized collectively through time as each contributes to the conversation of history, is one of the principal themes of *Rasselas*.

THE CHARACTER OF GOOD CONVERSATION

Beginning with the prince's fascination with Imlac's autobiography and continuing through the young travelers' interviews with those whom they meet along the way in their search for the happy choice of life, the drama of knowledge as ongoing conversation becomes their priority. Although they are interested in each other's subject matter, they come to recognize that communication is not merely subject matter but the circuit of that conversation as well and that the continuity of conversation both constitutes and gives evidence of the valuable connections among its participants. At several key moments in the story the continuity of conversation threatens to break down. These threats seriously endanger relations among the speakers. Imlac is an exemplary guardian of conversational continuity, not to be confused with simple agreement, ease, or even necessarily with mutual comprehension. He so values continuing a conversation that he will even swallow his pride in the face of an exasperated student. When, for instance, Rasselas interrupts his speech on the rigorous and unending education required to be a poet, remarking, "Enough! Thou hast convinced me, that no human being can ever be a poet," Imlac is more interested in continuing the dialogue than in defending himself. So he answers understatedly in a way that encourages the listener to reenter the conversation: "To be a poet is indeed very difficult" (YJ 16:46).

Later in the journey Nekayah expresses her serious suspicion of their teacher in a remark that threatens their conversation with complete breakdown. She remarks to her brother that Imlac seems not to favor their search for the happy choice of life, "lest we should in time find him mistaken" (YJ 16:89). For a student thus to suspect a teacher is extremely serious since learning requires trust. Students must be able to believe that their teachers unselfishly wish them well. But trust also includes accepting the possibility that students may sometimes find their teachers to be mistaken. The motive and intention behind the teaching are crucial to the mutual trust that underwrites successful education. Although Johnson understands such trust to be a precondition of education, he does not thereby take its existence for granted. Here in *Rasselas* he dramatizes a crucial moment of suspicion between student and teacher that could end their conversation. On several later occasions he shows the students affirming Imlac's teaching. These affirmations do not merely show that the poet was right all along. Rather they demonstrate the degree to which his students now trust him. The teacher's trustworthiness is far more crucial to education than his merely being right, for error, unlike untrustworthiness, does not undermine the entire activity and end the conversation.

If to the effects of suspicion are added the two motives that Johnson identifies in the *Life of Sir Thomas Browne* as usually accounting for why good minds fail to publish their discoveries (their sense that little is of sufficient interest to publish and the greater pleasure they take in inquiry than in publication), we can better measure the importance of conversation in *Rasselas*. It functions as the active assertion of meaning and participation against the many temptations to silence. Doing nothing is always a real possibility. And nothing, as Johnson repeatedly warns, annihilates the future by failing the present.

The recentering of the journey's formal significance in the establishment of a safe, ongoing conversation in which the participants come, though not without difficulty, to trust one another, is also anticipated by Rasselas's particular interest in the European postal system. Among all the various details that Imlac mentions about the world outside the happy valley, the description of the mails excites the prince most. His interest in this circuitry by which distant friends may come together hints at the terms of his insight later in the story when he alone urges the princess and Pekuah not to disguise themselves as travelers in distress in order to meet the mad astronomer. The women's intentions are not unkind, though they are motivated in no small part by curiosity. But the prince aptly identifies the serious error in their conception when he observes: "I have always considered it as treason against the great republick of human nature, to make any man's virtues the means of deceiving him, whether on great or little occasions. All imposture weakens confidence and chills benevolence" (YJ 16:158). To weaken confidence and chill benevolence are crimes against the community of trust upon which the possibility of communication depends, crimes nonetheless violent for not being physical.

This latter passage also recalls with added emphasis the scene where Nekayah discovers her brother and Imlac tunneling out of the valley. In addition, it anticipates the tale's increasing emphasis on the circuit, rather than the subject matter, of communication:

> He started and stood confused, afraid to tell his design, and yet hopeless to conceal it. A few moments determined him to repose on her fidelity, and secure her secrecy by a declaration without reserve. . . . The prince, who loved Nekayah above his other sisters, had no inclination to refuse her request, and grieved that he had lost an opportunity of shewing his confidence by a voluntary communication. (YJ 16:59, 60)

This passage offers a complex portrait of the mixed emotions typically arising from the drama of fear and regret—a drama all the more emphatic and compelling because it involves family relations. These relations, one feels instinctively, should serve as a model for the ideal operations of trustworthiness and generosity. Rasselas finds himself "afraid to tell his design, and yet hopeless to conceal it." His habitual training in secrecy in the happy valley clearly has had its effects.

When Nekayah next makes her case, she identifies precisely the elements of his fear and her good will that epitomize the theme of *Rasselas:* "Do not imagine," said the princess, "that I came hither as a spy. . . . not *suspicion* but *fondness* has detected you" (YJ 16:60, emphasis mine). The prince's response, combining public action with private recognition of his lost opportunity, is a simple but characteristically subtle example of Johnson's insight into how profoundly based in trust and confidence is the very possibility of human communication. In an essay on lying in *Adventurer* 50, Johnson cites Sir Thomas Browne's observation about the importance of truth to any joint undertaking: Even "the devils do not tell lies to one another; for truth is necessary to all societies; nor can the society of hell subsist without it" (YJ 2:362). The prince has not lied in a legalistic sense. But by acting out of suspicion and fear, by failing to trust and share knowledge with one whom he loves, he has missed an opportunity to contribute to the community of mutual reliance in a world filled with so many unavoidable divisions and disappointments. As the cumulative force of the story suggests, to let such an opportunity pass is always a mistake.

Rasselas's failure with his sister identifies how profoundly we are at risk with our intimates, an issue that recurs throughout the tale and one to which Johnson gives extended treatment in a later scene again between Nekayah and her brother. After the princess has completed her inquiry into married life, she reports to her brother, "if those whom nature has thus closely united are the torments of each other, where shall we look for tenderness and consolation?" (YJ 16:97). The very fact of such disappointment, however, identifies a source of particular energy, for in his characteristic way Johnson would have us recognize a vulnerability as a potential strength. But more precisely he would have us recognize what kinds of useful evidence about the interrelated operations of mind and feeling are to be discerned by examining the precise terms of such vulnerability.

The longest discussion in *Rasselas* is the debate on family life. In many ways the centerpiece of the tale, it is equally significant as a dramatization of the perils and possibilities of conversation, as two family members discuss the sociology of family. Nekayah's account to her brother ends with the report of contradictory findings on the question of whether it is better to marry early or late, and on whether celibacy or marriage is preferable. The prince points out his sister's self-contradiction: "You seem to forget," replied Rasselas, "that you have, even now, represented celibacy as less happy than marriage. Both conditions may be bad, but they cannot both be worst. Thus it happens when wrong opinions are entertained, that they mutually destroy each other, and leave the mind open to truth" (YJ 16:104). Though speciously accurate, the prince's criticism is needlessly unkind. When examined by standards more complex and appropriate to the matters being discussed than those he applies, they appear positively mistaken. Nekayah then points out to her brother his two interlinked errors, her manner offering a kind but firm corrective to his misplaced enthusiasm for logic. Each of Rasselas's errors involves a failure to accommodate ends to means aptly and economically.

The prince's quickness to point out his sister's error of logic phrased in absolutist terms expresses a philosophical attitude that regards the search for truth as a search for explanation only. If one considers a motive not to be something lying behind an act but rather the interweaving of value and event, then we can see the error in Rasselas's criticism. He begins with forensic condescension ("You seem to forget"), followed by the short sentences and the brusquely confident use of parallel structure ("Both conditions may be bad"), and the case-clinching use of causal logic ("Thus it happens") that includes a disturbingly violent expression ("mutually destroy each other"). His method assumes explanation (the charting of cause-and-effect relationships) to be the only legitimate form of knowledge. Thus Rasselas narrowly values what serves him well to believe.

Nekayah's answer critiques her brother's attack by noting the usefulness of a mode of knowledge (knowledge by acquaintance) different from the one he has so exclusively and insistently invoked. The style of her reply establishes not only the tone but also the terms of her model of understanding:

> "I did not expect," answered the princess, "to hear that imputed to falshood which is the consequence only of frailty. To the mind, as to the eye, it is difficult to compare with exactness objects vast in their extent, and various in their parts. Where we see or conceive the whole at once we readily note the discriminations and decide the preference:

but of two systems, of which neither can be surveyed by any human being in its full compass of magnitude and multiplicity of complication, where is the wonder, that judging of the whole by parts, I am alternately affected by one and the other as either presses on my memory or fancy? We differ from ourselves just as we differ from each other, when we see only part of the question, as in the multifarious relations of politicks and morality: but when we perceive the whole at once, as in numerical computations, all agree in one judgment, and none ever varies his opinion." (YJ 16:104–5)

Unlike her brother, the princess does not begin with accusation. She expresses surprise, thus introducing the element of subjectivity as an announced part of her method. Hers is not a narrowly private subjectivity but rather a consciously personal attitude and accompanying methodology that the rest of her speech will elaborate. It is an assertion about a manner of thinking (that is, perspectival) appropriate to certain kinds of inquiries. As such, it is quite different from her brother's ideal of objectivity. Nekayah's thinking capitalizes on precisely what would seem to be losses in a world that prizes objective, explanation-based, causal thinking. Expressing her emotional reaction first, rather than directly rebutting the prince with logic, she begins with a less confrontational, more invitational style typifying her model of personal knowledge. She is no less firm than Rasselas, but her firmness takes different, more intelligent and imaginative forms.

The princess's aim is not solely to clear the mind of contradictory opinions, thus leaving it open to truth. Instead, she draws a different picture, her emphasis falling not on the spatial but on the temporal qualities of thinking. Because she made her investigations of married and single life over time, there are temporal reasons for the contradictions in her findings. When the aim of knowledge is certainty, these qualities are admitted frailties. But as she now suggests, by identifying the admitted liability of temporal thinking, one gains valuable information for recognizing evidence and the shapes of satisfactory answers to be found on different kinds of searches. The princess's style exemplifies her counterclaims. Increasingly complex, always controlled, her thinking never fails to imagine and to take into account the other person's thinking, even if she disagrees with it. She begins in the first-person singular, then moves to the plural. Rasselas's remarks, by contrast, portray a drama of thought markedly different. This drama appears less directly associated with the speaker's *I* or the speaker's and audience's *we*. The pivots of his sister's invitational style are those places where she corrects her brother in a manner, by contrast with his flat-footed correction, that encourages their conversation to continue. Her gentle but acute question, introduced in the phrase, "where is the wonder?" characterizes a stance at once confident and generous—sufficiently confident to be generous. Nekayah's tactics are intelligent in larger and more encompassing ways than her brother's. They grant him the dignity he did not grant her. This maneuver is not merely a personal kindness, although for Johnson such kindness is scarcely negligible. Rather, in its form as personal kindness this act epitomizes the accurate operations of biographical thinking.

HOPEFUL COLLABORATION

The measure of Nekayah's success in introducing a new mode of thought is evident in her brother's reply. He adopts her tone and thus by implication her philosophical method, whose working assumption is the fact of human limitation and the need for collaboration in our inquiries:

> "Let us not add," said the prince, "to the other evils of life, the bitterness of controversy, nor endeavour to vie with each other in subtilties of argument. We are employed in a search, of which both are equally to enjoy the success, or suffer by the miscarriage. It is therefore fit that we assist each other. You surely conclude too hastily from the infelicity of marriage against its institution; will not the misery of life prove equally that life cannot be the gift of heaven?" (YJ 16:105–6)

Rasselas has learned from his sister's example, though he appears to be unaware of the source of this important new knowledge. The scene dramatizes a vision of learning as a cooperative endeavor from which we all stand equally to gain or lose. Hence our individual success is related to our success as members of a group. This episode serves as neither a simple rebuttal nor a mere alternative to but rather functions as a substantial enrichment of Rasselas's position. He is now beginning to think biographically. The scene began as a confrontation between a spatial model of truth based on explanation and a temporal model of truth based on acquaintance. It ends as a cooperative drama admitting and using the differences expressed by each speaker.

This episode, as should now be apparent, also serves an important retrospective function. From this new collaborative perspective we find ourselves in possession of new concepts in Rasselas's accumulating dictionary of pivotal terms that shed new light on all of the preceding conversations. The exchange between brother and sister identifies how much is at stake emotionally in performing one's chosen mode of thought. It is always risky business. Thus the participants' ultimate success in keeping their conversation going becomes, in the face of the odds against its success, a significant achievement.

With its efficient and happy resolution, this scene provides a backward glance at the earlier episode where Imlac discussed the ideal education of the poet and helps the reader appreciate more precisely the significance of his returning the conversation to Rasselas at the crucial moment when it seemed most in danger of breaking off. One cannot hope always for such successes. Nor should it be assumed that to continue a conversation is always better than to end it. Some conversations, like Imlac's discourse on poetry, or his and the prince's discussion of pastoral life, should end, if only for the moment. In this latter conversation, when Rasselas reports that he found these shepherds to be no happier than anyone else, he admits his fear that he may find no one who has made the happy choice of life. Hearing from Imlac new doubts and remarks that offer little comfort, the prince withdraws: "He therefore discoursed more frequently and freely with his sister, who had yet the same hope with himself, and always assisted him to give some reason why, though he had been hitherto frustrated, he might succeed at last" (YJ 16:89). Rasselas's instinctive response to retreat from his teacher's doubt may contain, from the reader's perspective, a degree of comic self-deception. But it is also a natural and not unhealthy response, a kind of emotional and intellectual survival instinct on the student's part. In order to continue, one must guard and nurture one's hopes.

Youth, as Johnson often observes, is the season for hopeful perseverance. Nekayah makes this same discovery in her inquiries into domestic happiness: "The colours of life in youth and age appear different, as the face of nature in spring and winter. And how can children credit the assertions of parents, which their own eyes show them to be false?" (YJ 16:96). The difference here defined is so often treated as a problem that the opportunity is lost for using it well. The misuse of differences most often occurs because a difference is assumed to be necessarily a problem. One notable contrasting example of the constructive use of difference occurs when Imlac decides to leave the happy valley and travel with the young people. Having lived in the world and subsequently withdrawn from it dissatisfied, he has no illusory hopes about what he may find the second time. But he can and does take accurate pleasure in watching his fellow travelers on their search. His repetition is thus genuine. While for the young people this trip is a first attempt, for Imlac it is a diverting variation on his first tour. This detail illustrates an artful and efficient conversion of difference into a ground of interest, rather than of suspicion or of fear.

From Johnson's point of view drawing the line between premature suspicion and naive receptivity always involves making subtle yet crucial discriminations so basic to survival that one cannot afford to blur them. Making these discriminations turns out to be rather more like the weaving of a semi-permeable membrane than the construction of a solid wall. His dramatization of the characters' attempts to keep a conversation going in *Rasselas*, sometimes succeeding, sometimes failing, is a case study in the functioning of such a membrane. The aim of conversation is to avoid both mere self-protection and territoriality, on the one hand, and injudicious acceptance, on the other. Johnson locates the model for cultivating such an ideal semi-permeability in Nekayah's recommendation that we recognize how "we differ from ourselves as we differ from each other." With this as the fundamental epistemological principle, autobiography and biography thus become the basis of the drama of education.

The example of how we differ from ourselves over time serves to familiarize us with the possibility that differing from others may not always be dangerous. There remains the fact that, since we generally learn from others or through their intermediation, we always at some level resent the inferiority implied by this inevitable structure of education. Hence we often learn less uneasily and more successfully from books and from the dead than from conversations with living people. Distant sources and dead teachers reduce the uneasiness of confrontation and humiliation which are nearly unavoidable when education takes place directly between people. But where there are liabilities, there are usually allied assets. The challenge is to see them. One of the benefits gained by the travelers comes simply from being together. For all their difficulties encountered throughout the journey, they still discover, when they return together to Cairo after ransoming Pekuah from the sheik, that they "were so well pleased at finding themselves together, that none of them went much abroad" [YJ 16:141]. Given the strains, suspicions, and failures that chronically plague human relationships, this single sentence implies success against great odds.

It is thus significant that *Rasselas* ends with the travelers coming together for a conversation. They repeat their ideal wishes at the end of the journey, now set in the notably more elaborate psychological context of the history of their travels. This setting is the drama of creativity, that delicate and permeable interrelation of hope, perseverance, and disappointment in their relations with themselves and others. The expression of their wishes followed by the seeming contradiction, "Of these wishes that they had formed they well knew that none could be obtained. . . . and resolved, when the inundation should cease, to return to Abissinia" (YJ 16:176), seems to function as a fairly straightforward comic deflation. Yet when set in the context of the mechanic flyer's reply to Rasselas's criticism of his project, "Nothing will ever be attempted, if all possible objections must be first overcome" (YJ 16:27), it takes on a different meaning. The man's project fails. But this failure does not invalidate the truth of his earlier remark, though it does italicize it and demonstrate once again how useful information may come at surprising times and from surprising sources.

Indeed, given their circumstances and resources, Rasselas, Nekayah, and Pekuah are more likely to succeed than the flyer. Johnson seems to have two related aims here in mind. One is a kind of crisscrossed structure of support, taking its strength from the intersection of stresses, strengths, and weaknesses. He places a useful general principle, a kind of skeptic's optimism, in the mouth of a figure involved in a wild project, and an optimist's pessimism in the minds of those with less unreasonable goals. Thus the general principles and projected practice intersect to produce a buttressing effect. This, in turn, provides a complex support enabling the reader's imagination to move in ways that would otherwise produce destabilizing oppositions. *Rambler* 2 describes this technique from another perspective:

> He that directs his steps to a certain point, must frequently turn his eyes to that place which he strives to reach; he that undergoes the fatigue of labour, must solace his weariness with the contemplation of its reward. In agriculture, one of the most simple and necessary employments, no man turns up the ground but because he thinks of the harvest, that harvest which blights may intercept, which inundations may sweep away, or which death or calamity may hinder him from reaping. (YJ 3:10)

The idea of an imagined future, like the idea of a pyramid, as Imlac discussed this subject with his fellow travelers, is no less real than either the acts performed to achieve that future or the actual pyramid itself, though each reality is differently constituted.

By noting how Johnson identifies such ordinary acts of the imagination that accompany, motivate, and solace our physical movement into the future, the distinctive quality of his insight into the sheer wonder of human achievement, however ordinary, can be discerned more precisely. Every individual human act lies on a continuum of the imaginative and the marvelous. Such a sense of the marvelous underwrites all the activity in *Rasselas*. That human beings achieve as much as they do never ceases to amaze Johnson. He was fascinated by the way achievement testifies to the dynamic interrelation between imagining a future and acting in a present integrally related to our past. In *Rasselas* he posits the importance of never taking this interrelation for granted, while in the *Lives of the Poets*, the subject of Chapter 6, he posits this inquiry as the primary impulse of biography.

Human beings are so constituted that this interrelation of imaginative cause and physical effect is the central principle of our existence, but one that, for any number of reasons, we often fail to live up to. Foremost among these reasons is our habit of placing events in the wrong categories. When, for instance, Imlac and Rasselas are digging a tunnel out of the happy valley, they work along slowly for some time with no perceptible progress. When the prince begins to feel discouraged, Imlac offers the following advice:

> Mark, however, how far we have advanced, and you will find that our toil will some time have an end. Great works are performed, not by strength, but perseverance: yonder palace was raised by single stones, yet you see its height and spaciousness. He that shall walk with vigour three hours a day will pass in seven years a space equal to the circumference of the globe. (YJ 16:58)

From this calculation based on the history of their efforts to date, combined with the analogy of how the palace was constructed, Imlac then extrapolates the probability of their future success. This pair of calculations is therapeutic for a chronically skeptical mind. Thus the present is defined from both directions by way of this imaginative exercise, which subsequently encourages the prince's current effort. The present now has a lively and present meaning composed of its relationship with the past and future.

When the pair begins to make faster progress, Rasselas names this progress "a good omen." Imlac now offers another revision of terms: "'Do not disturb your mind,' said Imlac, 'with other hopes or fears than reason may suggest: if you are pleased with prognostics of good, you will be terrified likewise with tokens of evil, and your whole life will be a prey to superstition. Whatever facilitates our work is more than an omen, it is a cause of success'" (YJ 16:59). This and the preceding correction are both directed toward exercising the prince's imagination in taking a healthy attitude toward the future and in understanding how such a stance is a function of our present being. *Rasselas* elaborates the full significance of *Rambler* 2: "This quality of looking forward into futurity seems the unavoidable condition of a being, whose motions are gradual, and whose life is progressive: as his powers are limited, he must use means for the attainment of his ends, and intend first what he performs last" (YJ 3:10). So much seems obvious. Yet oddly enough we seem to need constantly to rediscover the implications of this imperative, apparently inscribed so clearly in phenomena, for thought and action.

Imlac's first computational exercise gives Rasselas a basis for the closest thing to certainty one can hope for in the future, namely probable projection. Certainty, except in demonstrable reasoning, is a function of history and thus always an ex post facto determination. The second exercise also similarly contributes to a degree of stability and, like the first, requires accurate evaluation, which in this case is the naming of a past event, in other words, the writing of its history. The poet works systematically to keep the prince's imagination operating within a historical framework. Undue discouragement flies in the face of present evidence and of what one can reasonably know about the origins of any achievement. "Omens of good" are not admitted as cognitive categories within a historical framework. Such issues of naming are always important to Johnson, the lexicographer, for whom language was fundamentally related to ethics and action.

As beings whose movement toward the future is gradual and progressive and who must use ends to accomplish means, the choice between naming something an "omen" and naming it a "cause" distinguishes two radically different ways of sizing up the world. Appropriate naming has highly practical implications for action. Johnson, who lived in an age that valued accurate denomination, understood this fact and explored its significance more fully than most of his contemporaries. For Rasselas, susceptible as he is to fantasy, to name his means and manner of escape accurately makes a crucial difference in the probability of his success and in what he may hope to accomplish in the future created by that success.

Underlying his pervasive interest with people's actions in *Rasselas*, with how they come to do what they are now doing, with why they gave up what they used to do, or have resumed what they formerly abandoned, is Johnson's profound and wondering fascination with how things are done in this world and with how we achieve what we manage to achieve. This motif recurs throughout his work. Bate has identified how Johnson withheld himself from Swiftian irony, arguing that this characteristic act derives from his sense of responsibility to admit his participation in the collective condition of human error.[16] To this might be added an observation taking into account a more positive force in Johnson's imagination, one that directs him to maintain a stance of surprise and pleasure toward all achievement. *Rambler* 9 provides a useful concluding view of these matters:

> And it might contribute to dispose us to a kinder regard for the labours of one another, if we were to consider from what unpromising beginnings the most useful productions of art have probably arisen. Who, when he saw the first sand or ashes, by a casual intenseness of heat melted into metalline form, rugged with excrescences, and clouded with impurities, would have imagined, that in this shapeless lump lay concealed so many conveniencies of life, as would in time constitute a great part of the happiness of the world? (YJ 3:49)

Here Johnson notes how the study of history and, in particular, the study of the evidence of past success from modest beginnings define the good sense implicit in a stance of decent receptivity toward the work of others in the present. The historical record directs us probabilistically not to dismiss work that we do not as yet understand and to remain receptive to new ways of seeing the present and imagining the future.

The precondition for such a stance is ensured by our being wary of boredom. This preliminary alertness encourages the mind to exercise its natural fascination with history and to find for this fascination a full and accurate expression, like the travelers in *Rasselas* who repeat the stories of their own and other people's lives genuinely and with pleasure. Thus the real use of history,

---

16. Bate makes this argument in "Johnson and Satire Manqué."

Johnson believes, is not merely as a resource of edifying subject matter, or a collection of moral and immoral, successful and unsuccessful examples of behavior but rather as an exercise in assuming flexible, human attitudes in the present toward other people in the past, present, and future. History is a verb, not a noun.

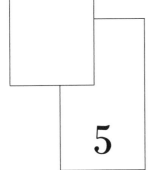

THE BIOGRAPHY
5 OF A NATION

*A Journey to the Western
Islands of Scotland*

AN INCESSANT SOLICITUDE FOR SOULS

F. Scott Fitzgerald once observed that "the test of a first-rate intelligence is the ability to hold two opposed ideas in the mind at the same time, and still retain the ability to function."[1] By now in this study it should be clear how and why, by Fitzgerald's definition, Johnson's intelligence is first-rate. The subtle yet practical insights composing his educational psychology and spiritual teleology in the Preface to *The Preceptor* and *The Vision of Theodore* define an orientation that, as I have now traced through the mid-1760s, continued to direct the work of his middle period.

The argument of the present chapter is best summarized in Johnson's description of Isaac Watts's effect on the reader:

> Whatever he took in hand was, by his incessant solicitude for souls, converted to Theology. As piety predominated in his mind, it diffused over his works. . . . it is difficult to read a page without learning, or at least wishing, to be better. The attention is caught by indirect instruction, and he that sat down only to reason is on a sudden compelled to pray. (LP 3:309)

In characterizing what he so admired in Watts's work Johnson also described what he aspired to and most valued in his own. And we, by considering Johnson's praise of Watts, for the way he catches our attention "by indirect instruction" so that we who "sat down only to reason" find ourselves "on a sudden compelled to pray," focus our attention on *A Journey to the Western Islands* (1775) as an exercise in writing the biography of a nation. In the *Journey* Johnson leads the reader by secular routes to spiritual truths.

1. *The Crack-Up with Other Uncollected Pieces*, 69.

Traveling in the Hebrides was for him a joyful occasion. He loved collecting new knowledge. It was also a humbling occasion when he came to narrate that knowledge in the form of a book. In the presence of objects that are truly and naturally great, like the lives of other people, their culture, and history—perpetual reminders of the separation between self and other—an author is rightly humbled. In the *Journey* Johnson narrates his unfolding sense of humility in the presence of such information. There turned out to be more, in several senses of the word *more*, than he could write about. He also came to understand the full implications of his responsibility to present the facts in such a way that his readers, who sat down only to reason, might find more than merely their rational powers engaged and more than simply their intellects educated.

In Chapter 1 of this study Johnson emerged as a man who could see the same things as, alternately, extraordinarily complex and radically simple. The difference depends on whether he chose to focus on ends or on means. While aware of how intricate human relations may be, he was equally conscious of the perfect simplicity characterizing our responsibility toward one another. "The most valuable things are those which are most plentifully bestowed," he writes in *Sermon* 15 (YJ 14:159). While in *Sermon* 24 he observes that "Providence has seldom made the same things necessary and abstruse" (YJ 14:257). Like his talent for harsh satire which, by restraining, he shaped into a more effective agent of moral instruction, his double vision yields similarly forceful results. It scans existence from two different viewpoints, each compelling, each necessary, each offering crucial equipment for living. His *Journey* applies this double perspective in a historical context involving real people. Travel, as fact and figure, appealed to him for at least three reasons: as a traditional emblem of the human condition, as a figure for the new empiricism, and as an exercise in imagining other people's lives.[2]

The quality and force of travel writing's appeal to him is suggested by one of the books from his Oxford days, *A Practical Discourse Concerning Death* (1689) by William Sherlock, dean of St. Paul's. Sherlock aims to teach the reader how rightly to value "what is not our own" and how to admire but not become mis-

2. Curley discusses the archetypal, intellectual, and moral aspects of the *Journey* in *Samuel Johnson and the Age of Travel*.

takenly attached to what is desirable but impermanent. To exercise readers in this discipline he offers the following anecdote:

> If then we must not entertain a Fondness for those Things which we cannot keep, let us in the next Place consider how we must use those Things which we have but a present and momentary Possession of: For Use is apt to beget a Fondness. Suppose then again, that in your Travels abroad, you pass thro' such a delightful Country; what is it that prevents your Fondness, but only considering that you are not at Home, that you must not always see and enjoy what you now do? And therefore all the fine Things you meet with, you rather look upon as Curiosities to be remarked in Story, or to be tried by Way of Experiment, or to be used for present Necessity, than as such Things which are to be enjoyed, which you know they are not.[3]

Unlike the episode of the young Johnson reading William Law and being overmatched by him, there is no account of his reaction to Sherlock. But it is not difficult to imagine how he might have reacted to this passage—how it might have caught and fired his imagination, and how he might have recalled it years later, less as material to be cited than as a way of conceptualizing his travels and of informing historical truth with spiritual meaning. Sherlock's insight makes the kind of sense Johnson particularly valued and was always alert to discover. His advice on how to avoid the spiritual self-delusion of mistaken fondness for the things of this world recommends approaching any experience or object with the same attitude one takes toward anything encountered on an actual journey. Right thinking, as here defined and as this notion also operates in Johnson's work, is not chiefly a matter of having the right ideas and desires but rather, since attitude directs action, of assuming the right attitude toward them. This distinction is, at one and the same time, subtle and highly practical.

The perspective of "present Necessity" that converts our gaze toward the world into "Curiosities to be remarked in Story" is, as already noted in Chapter 4, the perspective adopted by Imlac in order to make the happiness he could not otherwise find in the happy valley. This perspective similarly motivates his decision to take a second tour of the world with the young travelers and finally directs them to their inconclusive conclusion at the end of the journey. Undertaking his tour of the Hebrides Johnson applied these three orientations. In combination they give evidence of his canny

---

3. *Practical Discourse*, 7–8. Clifford mentions William Sherlock's book in *Young Sam Johnson*, 125.

epistemological insight that "there is no zero point" from which any inquiry can begin.[4] We can begin only from our presuppositions and beliefs, which is to say, we begin where we begin, and that beginning has a history, a specific character, an implied method. The true differences among our beginnings involve the varying degrees of consciousness brought to them.

LIFE AND LEARNING

The continuing popularity of the story about Johnson kicking the stone to refute Berkeley, whether cited to expose his limitations or to identify his insights, probably says as much about us, our fears, and our longings, as it says about him, perhaps more. In first "striking his foot with mighty force against a large stone, till he rebounded from it" and then remarking, "I refute it *thus*,"[5] he thrust his large, awkward body and his forcefully precise language into the gap of two of our deepest anxieties: about the reality of our being and of the world. This existential uneasiness has its material analogue in the scientific discovery discussed in *Rambler* 8: "Not only the great globes of matter are thinly scattered thro' the universe, but the hardest bodies are so porous, that, if all matter were compressed to perfect solidity, it might be contained in a cube of a few feet" (YJ 3:41). The incident also dramatizes our fear that, even if there is something out there, it may not connect with and respond to human beings. What would be the implications of feeling nothing when we kicked the stone or of not rebounding from it? For each of us, depending on how and what we define to be most at stake, it would be a different fear, several of which this study has already examined. Writers fear that their books will not be read;

4. John W. Wright, "Samuel Johnson and Traditional Methodology," 44. In *Samuel Johnson and the Age of Travel*, Curley discusses Johnson's travel writing in the context of "the mythic journey of everyman traveling from happy innocence to maturing experience on the downward path through the underworlds of evil and despair for his growth in wisdom and final ascent to some good" (42). Mary Lascelles discusses the place this book holds in his writings: "It is like the rest in the deliberate counterpoise of evidence, the structure of the argument. It is unlike, in the intensity of concern as to the outcome, and also in the fact of his own presence, however unobtrusively conveyed" (YJ 9:xv). Tomarken discusses "the interplay between history and autobiography" in the *Journey*, observing how this narrative "cannot be taken solely in mimetic terms as a fictionalized history of the Hebrides or merely as an autobiography. The interaction between the two is a literary representation of an historical process" ("Travels into the Unknown," 164).

5. Boswell, *Life*, 1:471.

teachers fear that their students will be unresponsive; students fear that their teachers will be treacherous, indifferent, or both. People generally prefer criticism, sometimes even pain, to annihilating silence. Some feeling is preferable to none at all. Silence and the absence of feeling signal the dangers of an unresponsive universe, an order of things involving the repeated loss of self with each expression.

Expression without response and the resulting erosion of the grounds of identity combine to bring about the death of hope, the most profound and precarious of all our ideas. Hope is not merely a state of mind but an active inquiry and the condition of imaginative possibility. Its continued existence depends on response. We are rightly frightened to think about the possibility of the world's being unresponsive because we know what this condition would mean. The conception and recognition of self depend, in other words, on getting something back each time we act or speak. Physiologically we depend on answers from the outside and on a body that can imagine no other possibility than dialogue. The senses continue to take our part conversationally with the world, as Hume so aptly recognized, conspiring to keep us sanely connected with that world, each sense simply taking for granted the relationship between the *in here* and the *out there*. As Johnson kicks the stone he makes a mock-encounter with hopelessness; hence the reason for this incident attracting us at a deep level. His action is a moving picture of the condition of our being, at one and the same time distinct from and fundamentally related to what surrounds us. When turned inward by self-consciousness, this physical geography becomes the material for those psychological topics of distance and contiguity, separation and union, having and losing, whose complementarity he so astutely examined throughout a lifetime of writing.

This image of Johnson and the stone attracts us, then, because here is someone thrusting himself into the gap of our fears about what is real and what is not. He exposes these fears as being simultaneously real and imaginary by reversing the Cartesian equation of cause and effect, between the *in here* and the *out there*. He actively proposes that one must assert the world in order to assert the self. He kicks the stone and rebounds from it. Identity reacts to a world. His reasoning through action, combined with language, returns to the actor to demonstrate the limits of language ("I refute it *thus*") as well as to express so-called common sense. Here actions and words speak equally loudly. People can tell themselves and other people only so much. Whether we are defining a language (in a dictionary) or telling the story of our own lives (in an autobiography), we always come up against this fundamental pair of opposites: the irreducibility of discourse to something simpler than itself and our inability to say everything we know. Similarly Johnson's habit of backing up to plant his foot hard on a step he had missed or to touch a post he had passed by is the expression of a mind drawn toward contemplating the world's unreality. Such movements are often read as aspects of his neurosis or superstition, as in part they may have been. But they are not reducible to mere symptomology. Together they enact a reaffirming, systematic choreography of reality. For these qualities of his thinking readers return to his works time and again to experience their psychosomatic reaffirmation.

Such perceptions on Johnson's part implicitly make a compelling case for a model of knowledge that is profoundly personal, which is not to say private. His functional theory of personal knowledge, an alternative to the paradigm of scientific objectivity, argues a case for human beings as assets, not liabilities in their own inquiries. It argues that present knowledge has a future and that this future is the self learning, which is to say, living. He thus proposes an alternative to Descartes's circuit of meaning. He does not merely deconstruct. His assertion that the world is a precondition of the self includes the complementary counterassertion that this circuit is completed only when we respond to that world. This position is sometimes mistakenly literalized. The *Journey* has been sometimes read as the work of "an extremely biased observer," an "Anglophile, Anglican, urban, learned philosopher-sophisticate" who "wears his 'philosophy' on his sleeve for us" and "did not take the Highland culture seriously."[6] This chapter argues the limitations of such criticism.

The *Life of Savage* (1744) gives a helpful preview of these assertions in the way it argues the impossibility of an autobiography by Savage. Johnson saw this deficiency as central to and revelatory of his subject's character, symptomatic of a pervasive flaw in the way Savage thought and thus in the way he could relate accurately both to himself and to others. Johnson's reading of Savage serves as evi-

6. Patrick O'Flaherty, "Johnson in the Hebrides: Philosopher Becalmed," 1991.

dence, once again, of how he believed that biography, whether written in the first or third person, is not narrowly speaking a genre but more largely a mode of inquiry and a manner of knowing:

> His mind was in an uncommon degree vigorous and active. His judgement was accurate, his apprehension quick, and his memory so tenacious that he was frequently observed to know what he had learned from others in a short time, better than those by whom he was informed; and could frequently recollect incidents with all their combination of circumstances, which few would have regarded at the present time, but which the quickness of his apprehension impressed upon him. He had the peculiar felicity that his attention never deserted him: he was present to every object, and regardful of the most trifling occurrences. He had the art of escaping from his own reflections, and accommodating himself to every new scene. (LP 2:429–30)

Savage was a man upon whom nothing and therefore paradoxically everything was lost. Because he was all attention, he remained child-like. Enthusiastic and insubstantial, he was the perennial student. He always sought to learn and was always learning. But his learning remained in the present tense, supplemented only by fortuitous, not systematic, recollections of the past and depictions of the future. Thus it was never completed and never became authentically his own. Because he neither filtered learning through an image of the future nor imagined a context in his present or future for what he was learning, he was never able to use his knowledge.

In his extreme, obsessive, and unsystematic efforts to learn, Savage gave a radical precedence to objects over the self, thereby losing his equilibrium with the world. Savage's psycho-pathology took the form of a self dissolving its boundaries and becoming coterminous with the present world. This dissolution has its appeal in the way it seems to relieve many anxieties about relations between self and other that Johnson repeatedly examines, particularly in the *Rambler*. At times he himself surely wished for a less intense awareness than he characteristically felt responsible for maintaining. But in Savage's life Johnson saw a fearful warning about the dangers of such letting go. What appears at first glance to be the rather benign error of over-sociability is actually a species of self-destructive solipsism and immaturity. Chronically undeveloped, Savage was a man for whom the present world was the self; thus, he was not on speaking terms with the world.

Yet the sheer unresisting quality of this man's mind remained fascinating to Johnson because of his abiding interest in the problem of attention in education. Here, in particular, his insights into his friend's problem as a species of learning disorder are of special interest to my line of inquiry. Savage learned with unresisting ease. But this ease masked a serious handicap in his ability to make real encounters with knowledge and to maintain his balance with the world. His excessive attention to the present is a parody of the creative principle that underwrites with special force the work of the second half of Johnson's career. This principle guides the individual's identity, the ongoing, developing structure of one's knowledge, in coming to terms with what it learns and not being overwhelmed by it. Savage was incapable of experiencing the abrasion, uncertainty, fear, and exhilaration of genuine encounters with knowledge. He failed to develop an accompanying principle of order and moral discrimination capable of sorting out what his attention registered all too completely. Johnson used his early insights into Savage's education gone wrong in dramatizing education first in *Rasselas* and second in the *Journey*. In both works he presents the experience of education as sometimes painful, always abrasive, and demanding of response.

Savage himself came to recognize the deadly results of failing to develop a principle for ordering his knowledge, a failure synonymous with immaturity. He insightfully describes a day that epitomizes the chaos of his life:

> The whole day has been employed in various people's filling my head with their foolish chimerical systems, which has obliged me coolly (as far as nature will admit) to digest, and accommodate myself to, every different person's way of thinking; hurried from one wild system to another till it has quite made a chaos of my imagination, and nothing done—promised—disappointed—ordered to send, every hour, from one part of the town to the other. (LP 2:421)

This scene distills the tragedy of Savage's life. His perfect attention, habitual accommodation, and subservience to things outside the self might seem to offer a solution to the experiences of division, suspicion, and fear that, as *Rasselas* compellingly dramatizes, inevitably accompany education. But as even Savage himself began to understand, by accommodating himself to "every different person's way of thinking," he was "hurried from one wild system to another" until his imagination became chaos. He failed to establish an accurate, dynamic equilibrium between the inner and outer worlds. Travel and travel writing, as this chapter will argue, served

Johnson as both figure and test case for precisely this significant exercise.

By now in this study it should be evident that Johnson understood education to be a risky business on many counts. Chief among these is the unavoidable fact that learning something new always involves encountering things not heretofore experienced in a language as yet incomprehensible. Hence we find ourselves required to negotiate our way among objects, signs, and meanings in a system that is inevitably new to us but which we must somehow comprehend in order to make our way among its individual elements. We learn, in other words, from wholes to parts. It is the only way possible. One aspect of Johnson's fascination with traveling in the Hebrides was his hope of finding there a nearly ideal situation for experiencing and recording these phenomena of learning—phenomena that typically include a troubling time lag among the three activities of seeing things and events, learning the appropriate language, and mastering meanings. Such an undertaking requires, on the part of the inquirer, storing different aspects of the foregoing information in anticipation of gathering the rest. Sometimes things are gathered without the language for them. Other times language is learned without the things. Still other times meaning is pursued without yet knowing its corresponding things or language. To be adept at gathering evidence (the parts making up a whole that must first be recognized before the parts make sense) requires a good eye for things invisible. In addition it requires patience and belief. Such belief manifests itself in the future-present tense that is the setting of all our inquiries.[7] To learn successfully requires our willingness to accept the gaps inevitably accompanying our learning—gaps from which may be inferred that hope is the basic structure of knowledge.

WHAT SCOTLAND OFFERED

Johnson loved his trip to Scotland because it was so full of things that impressed his mind with new images. He wrote home that he could not remember ever before having received so many new *ideas* (by which he means images) at one time. The trip also reversed the typical pattern of learning described in *Idler* 44. We usually collect images when we are young and distribute them when we are older.

7. William F. Lynch, *Images of Hope: Imagination as Healer of the Hopeless*, 123–25.

Learning occupies the first half of our lives, teaching the second. By reversing this pattern, his trip thereby rejuvenated him. Allowing him to collect new images, the tour made him once again a student. At the age of sixty-four he no doubt particularly enjoyed this feeling.

He liked the trip for another reason, too. The scenes offered his philosophic imagination an opportunity to finish a task left undone in the *Dictionary*. He could move on from the business of defining words to examining things and finally arrive at their actual meaning in life, though not by any such simple linear route as my phrasing would suggest. Not surprisingly, he was especially interested in the biographical meaning of things, which is to say their origin, relation to, and use in other people's lives. By pursuing these kinds of meaning he could become a poet of the real. In the Preface to the *Dictionary* he confesses the mock-serious dreams of a poet doomed to wake a lexicographer. The poet, he writes, would have finally arrived at things. When he had finished studying words, he hoped at last to come to the things themselves. Some eighteen years after the *Dictionary*, Johnson had the opportunity to put things first and thereby complete the earlier project. In the conclusion of the *Journey* he writes: "Such are the things which this journey has given me an opportunity of seeing, and such are the reflections which that sight has raised." In the sense identified here, the *Journey* constitutes a sequel to the earlier work. The lexicographer arrives at the referents and becomes a poet of the things of other people's lives.

In another way, too, this later work completed the earlier undertaking. Both a dictionary and a travel narrative compile large amounts of material. "A Dictionary consists of independent parts, and therefore one page is not much a specimen of the rest."[8] Furthermore, he observes in his preface to Macbean's *Dictionary of Ancient Geography* (1773):

> As Dictionaries are commodious, they are likewise fallacious: he whose works exhibit an apparent connexion and regular subordination cannot easily conceal his ignorance, or favour his idleness; the completeness of one part will show the deficiency of another: but the writer of a Dictionary may silently omit what he does not know; and his ignorance, if it happens to be discovered, slips away from censure under the name of forgetfulness. (PD 135)

8. Johnson, *The Letters of Samuel Johnson: With Mrs. Thrale's Genuine Letters to Him*, 2:434.

By its very structure, a dictionary allows the writer to conceal certain aspects of his ignorance from the reader and even from himself. A travel narrative, on the other hand, by attempting to connect, order, and show the relations among the parts of a large body of materials, exposes its author to uninterrupted and undisguisable risks. Each part of the *Journey* is a specimen of the whole. It thereby continuously measures the author's competence—a competence all the more critically at stake when one attempts to make connections among real things relating to real people's lives.

These materials, lives and the things of people's lives, are biographical. They require of the writer a particular deference and respect, as well as a full account of his knowledge and his ignorance. At the same time, because these materials are biographical, they prescribe a method relying fundamentally on the writer's personal knowledge, on his model of the nature of things, on the way he connects one thing with another, and on the way he envisions the whole he is constructing. Johnson's method has been described in our century by Maurice Merleau-Ponty: "I do not so much perceive objects as reckon with an environment."[9] Only life can make sense of other lives. This is the biographical horizon of thinking, its extent as well as its limit. As Johnson travels, he explores the many possibilities such thinking offers for testing our resilience when faced with the fact that we often differ not only from others but also from ourselves over time and for applying the implications of this existential fact for understanding history.

Johnson regularly refers to himself throughout the *Journey,* but these references are more than merely personal. They describe the larger context that not only encompasses the circumstances and conditions of his learning but also extends substantially beyond them. This complex of references constitutes his philosophic method. They accumulate into the dramatic example of a person learning and subsequently passing on that knowledge to others. He alludes, for instance, to his career as a writer, to his work on Shakespeare, to his deciding to write this book, to being a city-dweller, to having an English eye for landscape. He confesses his likes and dislikes. Such personal references go to show in real life what *Rasselas* had earlier demonstrated in fiction, namely that some desire is necessary to keep life in motion. The desiring eye is the seeing eye. Accuracy is grounded in desire and interest. Out of his image of the

9. *Phenomenology of Perception*, 416.

world, including a self-image, Johnson asks questions, predicts answers, and makes mistakes. Sometimes he fails to find satisfactory answers and often he must revise his expectations to accommodate unexpected discoveries.[10]

Moving asymptotically toward the truth, he dramatizes the activities of communication and response, the examination of consistency of thought, and the survival value of ideas as the foundation for the orderly, reliable growth whether of a nation (Scotland), of a writer (himself), or of anyone reading the book.[11] Such are the organizing principles of the narrative. These principles challenge us to say what we know but sometimes find too powerful to admit about the deeply personal nature of all our inquiries. These principles, too, organize our lives when we chart a course midway between the extremes of experiment and mechanism, on the one hand, revelation and vitalism, on the other, by asserting the methodology of personal knowledge.[12] This methodology is as demanding as it is rewarding. It requires first and last a commitment to the truth of efficiency, as Johnson distinctively defines that truth to mean being true to time.

He establishes the importance of truth to time on the first page of the *Journey* by foregoing the opportunity to give an easy, conven-

10. Francis R. Hart discusses Johnson's preoccupations with problems and methods of perception and description ("Johnson as Philosophic Traveler: The Perfecting of an Idea"); Donald T. Siebert, Jr., discusses how "Johnson is determined to show how eagerly men embrace pleasing delusions and by contrast how difficult it is to see things as they are" ("Johnson as Satirical Traveler: *A Journey to the Western Islands of Scotland*," 138).

11. Kenneth E. Boulding discusses this method in *The Image: Knowledge in Life and Society*, 174. Of the work on the *Journey* from this perspective, of particular interest are: Thomas Jemielity, "Dr. Johnson and the Uses of Travel," particularly his remarks about how "the principles of its [traveling's] attraction for Johnson are consonant with those that impel him to the world of letters" (459); John B. Radner, "The Significance of Johnson's Changing Views of the Hebrides," who proposes that the author's revisions of the *Journey* "suggest that while Johnson learned much while making his trip, he also learned much while writing about it" (134); and Edward Tomarken, "A Historico-Literary Text: Samuel Johnson in Scotland," who argues the distinction between Johnson's book and both Pennant's and Martin's traditional *Tours* and Boswell's journal. "Johnson," Tomarken suggests, "appropriates the description of externals from the tour and the personal impressions from the journal: the combination is new in kind" (24).

12. Lascelles remarks on Johnson's "presence" in the *Journey*, that "the ideas burn, as in the heart of a fire, and are communicated in a manner he uses nowhere else" and that "the particulars are part of the author's own unfolding experience" (YJ 9:xv, xxvii).

tional, but unnecessary description of Edinburgh. This city, he remarks, is too well known to require description. He proceeds instead to describe the small rocky island, Inch Keith, just off-shore. He and his companions explored the tiny mass with dispro-portionate seriousness, looking for signs of habitation, datable remains of its history, and opportunities for restoration. These top-ics anticipate the travelers' later substantial investigations and thus allow them to mock-encounter with their future work. This description of Inch Keith can, of course, hardly compare with the description of Edinburgh Johnson could have written. Had he writ-ten this description, he would have avoided being criticized by readers who interpreted this omission of Scotland's greatest city as typical English prejudice. But Edinburgh did not need to be described yet again, and Johnson does not tell a lie about what needs to be done merely in order to plump his book or protect him-self against anticipated criticism. Nor by describing Edinburgh does he waste the reader's time and thus steal what can never be replaced. Such honesty and economy exemplify the workings of a healthy imagination, one that values efficiency over self-display and regards the reader as a real and indispensable participant in the author's work.

As he tries to obtain accurate information from the inhabitants, he must again reckon with problems regarding truth that accumu-late and interconnect along the way as his perspective changes. As he travels, his focus alters from an original single aim of gathering *the truth* to a manifold and encompassing one of trying to under-stand why he is being given what appears to be outright false and contradictory information. As this shift occurs, Johnson develops a different kind of philosophical inquiry from the one with which he began. Although he does remain interested in gathering accurate information about the inhabitants' lives, he becomes increasingly and finally encompassingly interested in understanding the logic that generates their accounts.

Issues of truth and honesty emerge not only as synchronic prob-lems with psychological subtleties but also as diachronic ones with historical complications. Truth, so Johnson discovers, usually has no single history. The larger issue here at stake is that of repre-sentation, the power we grant to language to speak of our world. As the trip proceeds, he becomes less interested in rigidly and nar-rowly questioning Highland information in terms alien to it. He attempts increasingly to discover the logic of the inhabitants' accounts of their region and their lives. This inquiry into the system generating the performance of their accounts anticipates the way he would attempt to understand the logic of metaphysical poetry in the *Life of Cowley*, written at the end of the decade. Scotland turned out to have been a test case for this later study, for here he learned to ask the kinds of questions he later applied to the metaphysicals—"What would account for anyone's writing such poetry?"—just as earlier he had inquired into why the inhabitants of the Hebrides tell stories as they do.

As the journey in *Rasselas* begins in empirical inquiry and develops into a therapeutic epistemological investigation, so here the traveler reimagines his investigative givens and priorities. The imagination capable of suspending its presuppositions and absolutes in order to attempt to understand the Highlanders' values gives evidence of a mind that values conversation over inquisition and recognizes that keeping a conversation going is often worth substantial sacrifice. This activity also anticipates the ability rightly to acknowledge debts and to invent virtuous acts without models or precedent.

Two-thirds of the way through the *Journey*, Johnson offers the following analysis of truth as a historical and psychological composite:

> The inhabitants knowing the ignorance of all strangers in their language and antiquities, perhaps are not very scrupulous adherents to truth; yet I do not say that they deliberately speak studied falsehood, or have a settled purpose to deceive. They have inquired and considered little, and do not always feel their own ignorance. They are not much accustomed to be interrogated by others; and seem never to have thought upon interrogating themselves; so that if they do not know what they tell to be true, they likewise do not distinctly perceive it to be false. (YJ 9:117)

Truth is a function of knowledge and a result of practice in self-consciousness and self-interrogation. Johnson considers how his own notions of truth and falsehood, notions that he necessarily brings to this inquiry, may be not eternal and self-evident propositions but instead historically constructed categories invented over years of cultural practice. Johnson is, to be sure, an empiricist. But he is also a perspectivist (as distinct from a relativist) who, as he travels through the Hebrides, sincerely poses the questions: "How and why would people speak this way?" and "What might account for it?" As he attempts to understand the Scots' narrative habits, which it would be inadequate simply to call lying, he simultaneously emphasizes his subjectivity. He underscores his identity as outsider and the need to render this subjectivity semi-permeable to other people's minds and lives by attempting to imagine how and why the Scots think and speak as they do.

The degree of this semi-permeability increases throughout the trip. This increase, far from blurring the boundary between subject and object, produces a more nuanced and satisfying portrait of their distinctions and interrelations. Early in the tour, for instance, he recounts the contradictory information given him about brogues, the kind of shoe worn in the Highlands. On a single day and in the same house he was told that brogue-making was a domestic art and also a trade. He comments on this contradiction: "But such is the laxity of Highland conversation, that the inquirer is kept in continual suspense, and by a kind of intellectual retrogradation, knows less as he hears more" (YJ 9:51). At this stage of the journey the traveler's primary aim is to gather factual information about Highland life. But by the time he makes the historical analysis of truth, which allows for the Highlanders' different consciousness of truth and falsehood, his balance of interest has shifted from the empirical to the epistemological. The passage on brogues defines its subject more narrowly as the difficulty of getting accurate information, while the later passage identifies the multi-layered issues of historical and cultural definitions of truth. Thus Johnson deconstructs the notion of truth as a unitary and natural concept. He relocates it in the flux of time and space. But in so doing he neither makes the concept completely relative nor condescends to the Scots.

When he arrives at Rasaay, he takes the occasion to comment on the Scots historian, Martin Martin. Although he finds fault with Martin's work, his criticism is not narrow. He does not make the mistake Rasselas made with Nekayah in their discussion of married life. Rather, as with the Scots he interviewed, he attempts to imagine how and why Martin did what he did:

> Martin was a man not illiterate: he was an inhabitant of Sky, and therefore was within reach of intelligence, and with no great difficulty might have visited the places which he undertakes to describe; yet with all his opportunities, he has often suffered himself to be deceived. He lived in the last century, when the chiefs of the clans had lost little of their original influence. The mountains were yet unpenetrated, no inlet was opened to foreign novelties, and the feudal institutions oper-

ated upon life with their full force. He might therefore have displayed a series of subordination and a form of government, which, in more luminous and improved regions, have been long forgotten, and have delighted his readers with many uncouth customs that are now disused, and wild opinions that prevail no longer. But he probably had not knowledge of the world sufficient to qualify him for judging what would deserve or gain the attention of mankind. The mode of life which was familiar to himself, he did not suppose unknown to others, nor imagined that he could give pleasure by telling that of which it was, in his little country, impossible to be ignorant. (YJ 9:64–65)

As in the discussion of Cowley and the metaphysicals whose poetry he found faulty, Johnson does not criticize without attempting to enter into the intelligence he is criticizing. He imagines a logic to account for Martin's collecting so little information about his country that has proved to be of subsequent interest or use. Describing Martin's situation and trying to account for his failure, he defines a paradoxical territory of responsibility, with its accompanying inevitable blindness, within which all writers, to greater or lesser degree, work. Martin can legitimately be held accountable by his readers for knowing more than he possibly could have known.

Johnson begins by noting Martin's qualifications for the task he failed to perform. Though he could read and was in the right place at the right time, "yet he suffered himself to be deceived." This failure is his readers' loss. They can now never know with certainty or in any detail "a series of subordination and a form of government," "uncouth customs," and "wild opinions" that would have given pleasure to readers from "more luminous and improved regions." What is lost is certain. It now remains to be considered what may be accomplished in its aftermath. By detailing the author's failure and our subsequent loss, Johnson refers simultaneously to the past and the future. By describing what was left undone, he sketches an agenda for a future where it may be hoped such losses will not be repeated. As for why Martin failed as a historian, the reason seems clear; he was insular. Knowing too little of the world, he could not imagine what might be of interest to people other than himself and his contemporaries. He did not know in a sense sufficiently large how he differed from others.

As in the instances of Johnson's analysis of lying, here too he subtly notes error in ways that open out onto more and larger issues than the initial incident might have predicted. Perhaps especially when reading the *Journey*, one feels renewedly the force of Montaigne's observation that the soul is served usefully by error. The terms of this useful service always include the assertion of responsibility for failure. By granting a crucial measure of free will, this assertion also grants a measure of dignity to those who failed. Johnson often asks of us the seemingly impossible: to know what we do not yet know and to be aware of what our circumstances do not readily make available to us. But he makes these demands precisely because he understands that learning by its nature and structure occurs in the context and through the agency of precisely such seeming impossibility of imagining an as yet indistinct future. Martin's failure is perfectly comprehensible. In some ways it would have been more surprising if he had succeeded in writing a full account of his country. But if there were no exceptions to plausible or even probable failure, we would know very little of the world and expect even less of ourselves.

Johnson's revised notions of truth and accountability are accompanied by another transformation during the course of the journey. He increasingly encourages the Scots to study their own nation and thus to carry on and complete Martin's work. In so doing he brings to natural philosophy his understanding of the compelling psychological and ethical differences between the genres of biography and autobiography. Both kinds of life histories are agreeable and useful. But of the two, the first-person story is always more valuable. Autobiography is closer to the truth in its complex, manifold, and ambiguous identity. Johnson, as traveler in the Hebrides, gathers materials for the biography of a nation. The biographical traveler's ongoing lesson to Scotland is that the Scots should study themselves and thereby use their past as a transition to a more effectual future.

UNDERSTANDING THE SCOTS

The discussion so far in this chapter could be summarized by reinvoking Wittgenstein's insight that understanding is no single or unitary experience but rather a family of experiences. Understanding is an experience of recognizing and discriminating, by their various criteria, the family of events known, in turn, as understanding. As is always the case with names and categories, there is a fundamental circularity. Different kinds of writing represented and functioned for Johnson as different kinds of understanding. Autobiography, though related to, is different from and superior to biography. In the same way, the Scots' account of their own nation would be different from and superior to narratives any non-Scot could write. Each embodies a distinctive kind and quality of understanding. But the former is, in each instance and if done well, more valuable. It follows that for foreign travelers, as for biographers, this insight implies the necessity of cultivating humility as part of their methodology.

While Johnson is emphatic in his opinions, an aspect of the *Journey* interpreted by some readers as prejudice, he does not in fact raise his opinions above Scotland and the Scots. He is fundamentally humble in the presence of such significant objects, recognizing the limits of the biographer's consciousness that, like the literary critic's, must assent to its subordinate status relative to the objects it studies. If he is ever in danger of forgetting his position, experience conspires to remind him. When, for instance, he compliments one of his hosts on his speech, he notices "that I did not please him: I praised the propriety of his language, and was answered that I need not wonder, for he had learned it by grammar" (YJ 9:36). When he asks another man why so many Highlanders have chosen to emigrate and "whether they would stay at home, if they were well treated," he is rightly reprimanded with the reply "that no man willingly [leaves] his native country" (YJ 9:38). Johnson immediately comprehends the complex but self-evident significance of this correction.

The Highlander's reply marks the typical limits of the traveler's imagination, the point at which he conventionally errs by over-assuming the otherness of other people and by allowing his objectivity thereby paradoxically to lead him astray. But it also marks the place where the traveler as biographer may assume autobiographical knowledge as a resource for his inquiries. Johnson discovers both of these truths on his journey. In gathering certain kinds of information, he goes astray by assuming the rules of evidence of a literate, rather than an oral, culture. Here he must revise his methods and assumptions in order to be a historian in terms suggested by the continuing orality of Hebridean history. As he comes to recognize that every thing in those countries has a history, he perceives that "narrations like this, however uncertain, deserve the notice of a traveller, because they are the only records of a nation that has no historians, and afford the most genuine representation of the life and character of the ancient Highlanders" (YJ 9:50). Narrations such as this one are at odds with writing. And since writing was one of the principal achievements of Johnson's culture, as well as an activity that defined his life, he naturally felt a degree of foreignness, perhaps even estrangement by virtue of this difference between his culture and the Scots'. Certainly he recognized that this difference had implications for his investigation.

But if his question about emigration evokes a stern correction, it is not thereby shown to be foolish or inaccurate. Nor do Johnson's comments about an oral culture suggest that his presuppositions, even though they lead him into error, would be better left unsaid. The question could scarcely go unasked because the traveler sees and must question phenomena that do not occur in his native land. The inevitability of his questions marks the first stage of the compressed and multi-layered education provided by his trip but available only through active questioning that is sometimes apt, sometimes bumbling. While some of the answers he receives may make him feel ashamed or chagrined, all of them initiate him into knowledge by acquaintance. In order to gather such knowledge by acquaintance Johnson sometimes tries to imagine how he, as traveler, appears to the natives and how that appearance shapes their response to him:

> I did not meet with the inquisitiveness of which I have read, and suspect the judgment to have been rashly made. A stranger of curiosity comes into a place where a stranger is seldom seen: he importunes the people with questions, of which they cannot guess the motive, and gazes with surprise on things which they, having had them always before their eyes, do not suspect of any thing wonderful. He appears to them like some being of another world, and then thinks it peculiar that they take their turn to inquire whence he comes, and whither he is going. (YJ 9:103)

By imagining how a traveler is perceived by the natives of the land he visits, he illustrates how strangeness is always mutual. The traveler and the native are equally foreign and perplexing to one another.

The invaluable resource of knowledge available in such encounters is best defined in the following observation: "In countries like these, the descriptions of famine become intelligible" (YJ 9:138). The way that traveling in the Hebrides makes famine intelligible is similar to the way that the innkeeper's reply to Johnson's question about emigration made that phenomenon intelligible. Intelligibility, as defined cumulatively throughout the *Journey*, is a knowledge not *about* or *of* but *through* a subject. Such knowledge does not merely complete the dictionary definition of a word; it makes that knowledge different. The difference between first- and second-hand knowledge, as the *Journey* demonstrates, is more than simply a matter of degree. Throughout the *Journey* meaning becomes an increasingly resonant and resonating experience.

The significance of an idea's becoming intelligible resides partly in the way such knowing marks simultaneously the powers and limitations of language. This distinction becomes apparent when we consider how Johnson typically alternates lengthy expository passages in the *Journey* with brief passages, such as the remarks about famine and emigration. His readers thereby forcefully experience the effects of different kinds of knowledge, some that enter consciousness by degrees, educating and accustoming us slowly, others that enter and capture the mind almost instantaneously. He proposes, for instance, a consideration of the different meanings of the word *shop* in London and in the Hebrides, respectively:

> To a man that ranges the streets of London, where he is tempted to contrive wants for the pleasure of supplying them, a shop affords no image worthy of attention; but in an island, it turns the balance of existence between good and evil. To live in perpetual want of little things, is a state not indeed of torture, but of constant vexation. I have in Sky had some difficulty to find ink for a letter; and if a woman breaks her needle, the work is at a stop. (YJ 9:130)

This contextual definition of *shop* within the drama of social activity renews our attention to and interest in this most ordinary of words. He makes the word intelligible by defining it in two different cultural contexts.

In each context the word and the phenomena to which it refers function and take their meaning relative to an entire cultural scene and to the expectations operating locally as the ground of perception. In England a shop could never function to turn "the balance of existence between good and evil." But being part of a different and much more limited system of life in the Hebrides, it does make precisely this crucial difference here. A broken needle that means little in England because there are many shops where needles can be purchased, means in the Hebrides that a woman cannot continue her work. A similar situation exists with ink and the difficulty of finding it. For Johnson, as writer, this lack was particularly noticeable since it affected him materially. In three sentences he has defined shop functionally within a system of living. Thus with telling specificity, he makes island life intelligible from the inside out. His method also implies the significance of the ordinary, even trivial, detail in writing the life of a nation, just as in writing the life of an individual.[13]

He introduces this activity of definition in the opening paragraph of the *Journey* where he describes the travelers' "first experiment of unfrequented coasts," a small island just off Edinburgh. Mock-encountering with the archaeological techniques and historical methods they will be using through the travels to come, they examine the ruins of a deserted fort. As they leave the island, he remarks:

> We left this little island with our thoughts employed awhile on the different appearance that it would have made, if it had been placed at the same distance from London, with the same facility of approach; with what emulation of price a few rocky acres would have been purchased, and with what expensive industry they would have been cultivated and adorned. (YJ 9:4)

The logic of these comments recurs throughout the journey, their tone growing increasingly serious. In his examination of the fort he experiments fancifully by imagining the repercussions of transporting these few acres from one geography, governed by its distinctive economic system, to another; he then imagines the financial implications of this imagining. The same property, if located just offshore London, would signify something quite different financially. The laws of supply and demand define land differently in different places. While this may seem obvious once said, it does not thereby go without saying. Achieving such insights and rendering them intelligible are among the chief purposes of Johnson's trip and a primary aim of his account.

---

13. Maximillian E. Novak makes the connection between Johnson's insight into the importance of examining the details of "ordinary" existence in the writing of literary history in the *Lives of the Poets* and in travel writing in the *Journey* in his essay, "Johnson, Dryden, and the Wild Vicissitudes of Taste" when he remarks: "Johnson writes well on Dryden because his literary history is infused with an understanding that there can be no history of poetry or the drama that is separated from ordinary existence, because he could take the time to examine the nature of windows in a hut around Banff in Scotland and explain that such a small matter might be the key to the entire society" (71). Thomas Jemielity comments on how Johnson's analysis makes the Highlands come alive "in a way impossible from a mere guidebook approach" and on how he gives "attention to those particularities which will render this society more intelligible" (" 'More in Notions than in Facts': Samuel Johnson's *Journey to the Western Islands*," 324).

His notion of intelligibility recalls the issue earlier discussed of the way a case gathers throughout the *Journey* for how and why understanding cannot be considered a single act or activity but rather must be recognized as a family of experiences with distinct, if complex, characteristics. The figure for the drama of this developing sense on Johnson's part is his discussion of second sight. Both Johnson and Boswell were particularly interested in investigating the accounts of this phenomenon, but they failed either to verify or to disprove it. His reflections demonstrate how he locates second sight within a field of related experiences: "Considered in itself, it involves no more difficulty than dreams, or perhaps than the regular exercise of the cogitative faculty" (YJ 9:109). Identifying this extrasensory perception as part of a continuum of mental activity in turn illustrates one of the chief characteristics of his mind, namely the way he revises the notion of definition. He revises the conventional meaning as an activity of marking and limiting into one of locating and juxtaposing elements that collectively describe a pattern of intelligibility. Of all of his writings the *Journey* most lucidly and compellingly embodies and explores this idea. This pattern is similar to Wittgenstein's description of the experience of understanding and what it feels like. Everyone knows how it feels to pass from what we know to what we do not know, from the familiar to the unfamiliar. We also recognize the family of experiences that constitutes becoming familiar with the unfamiliar. For Johnson such movements of a mind becoming acquainted with the unfamiliar and approximating the unknown were always fascinating. For him such experiences were, in equal parts, wondrous and commonplace, as his remarks on the possible likeness of second sight, dreams, and thinking suggest.

His notion of intelligibility converges with his working concept of personal knowledge. Travel served him as a particularly apt occasion for inquiring into and dramatizing the deeply personal nature of all our knowledge. Johnson did not take for granted the commonplace about how travelers see and learn only as much as they take with them on their journey. His dramatization of how he learned from his travels substantially modifies the Lockean idea of the observer as chiefly a receiver of impressions. It depicts the traveler instead as one who, for better or worse, is conditioned by personal knowledge in the search for intelligibility.

As lexicographer, Johnson is an acute and wittily serious representative everyman and woman, one who has defined the language in order to make it an instrument less liable to decay. As travel writer, he set out to discover in the Scots' system of life the biographical intelligibility of words like *famine* and *shop*, and of concepts like *hope*, which seem alternately so fragile and so strong in light of the variety of his experiences. He learns of an estate overwhelmed by sand and utterly lost. He is informed of the death by drowning of the young Laird of Col, and he visits Mr. Braidwood's college for the deaf and dumb in Edinburgh, palpable proof of how "one of the most desperate of human calamities [is] capable of so much help" (YJ 9:164). Such examples and others like them surely interested him not just as information about but as thresholds opening onto the terrible and wonderful aspects of other people's lives. Such a view of the relationship between the *Dictionary* and the *Journey* contributes to the revision of Johnson's mistaken reputation as a conservative. As there is always an appeal from criticism to life, so the trip to Scotland demonstrates that there is always a similar appeal from lexicography to life.

His familiar concluding remarks identify the author's autobiographical liabilities and assets. As a visitor to Scotland, he considers both from a sociological perspective:

> Having passed my time almost wholly in cities, I may have been surprised by modes of life and appearances of nature, that are familiar to men of wider survey and more varied conversation. Novelty and ignorance must always be reciprocal, and I cannot but be conscious that my thoughts on national manners, are the thoughts of one who has seen but little. (YJ 9:164)

Here he depicts himself, describing his characteristic threshold of perception as traveler. Yet as the *Journey* cumulatively argues, the author's thinking cannot be reduced to the sum of these characteristics. Nor is this thinking the "effect" of certain "causes." He would reduce neither thought nor action to the mere result of a finite and predictable series of previous events. The *Journey* gives evidence of how whatever a traveler takes with him may condition but need not limit or even necessarily predict what he will find, because no simple model of cause and effect is adequate to explain this drama. The *Journey* also gives evidence of how, more generally considered, thinking itself is in equal parts both ordinary and wonderful.

The model for this paradoxical account of learning is his journey into unknown territory. An increase of understanding, as distinct from the mere addition of facts with the same degree of intelligibility as the information one already possesses, can neither be demonstrated certainly, accounted for logically, nor explained causally. Furthermore it never has to happen. Genuine learning is no accident, but neither is it fully predictable. The *Journey* is perhaps Johnson's most self-conscious meditation on this subject. The products of such a mind are always as startling as they are new and renewing. They hold us in a pleasing captivity to the possibility of renovating history, and thus for living meaningfully in the present by adopting and adapting what we learn in the present and inherit from the past into a set of questions and propositions distinctively our own and hence material for our future.

6 | WRITING LIVES

Lives of the English Poets

THE PERSONAL POSSESSION OF HISTORY

Chapter 4 considered *Rasselas* as Johnson's dramatization of history, as a kind of conversation about one's own and other people's lives. Chapter 5 considered *A Journey to the Western Islands* as his experiment in writing the biography of a nation. Becker's analysis of the false analogy often drawn between the moral and physical worlds provides a useful summary of these ideas in preparation for turning to the *Lives of the Poets*:

> Desiring to gain control over nature, the scientist is little concerned with any actual concrete situation, whereas the historian, aiming to appropriate the experience of the past for himself and his fellows, is concerned precisely with the concrete human world, not as it might be under certain conditions but as it has actually been. The difference is radical. It is for this reason that *although scientific knowledge, through its formulae, can be practically applied, to the great benefit of all men, knowledge of history cannot be thus practically applied, and is therefore worthless except to those who have made it, in greater or lesser degree, a personal possession.*[1] (emphasis mine)

To this might be added George Santayana's version of the same insight in his remark that history gives a gift of great interest to the heart.[2] Johnson, too, knew that we learn history differently from the way we learn science. Only life can make sense of another life. Thus it follows that biography is a radical propaedeutic to history.

Readers of Johnson's *Lives* have generally charted two related courses in reading these biographies. One is the direction proposed

---

1. "A New Philosophy of History," review of *The Interpretation of History* by L. Cecil Jane, 148.
2. Cited in Becker, "Everyman his own Historian," 235.

by William R. Keast in his important essay, "The Theoretical Foundations of Johnson's Criticism." He describes Johnson's conception of literature as "a mode of activity, as one of the things men can do."[3] Succeeding critics, as for instance notably, Damrosch and Folkenflik, have developed implications of this proposal as they bear upon the ways he evokes the past by characterizing it in terms of human activity.[4] In a related manner Bate and Wain have discussed how the *Lives* rescue and give voice to the dead. Wain observes that "at every turn he comes upon some once familiar ghost." Bate comments that from Johnson's way of writing about the English poets "we sense an instinctive desire to rescue them, if only briefly, from extinction in the sludge of time: to see them as part of the general drama of human effort, experience, risk, hope, and disappointment; to evaluate them as lives—as experiences in living."[5]

In her revision of the presuppositions of nineteenth-century biography for the twentieth century, Virginia Woolf looked to the eighteenth century for her model and inspiration. In the essay "I am Christina Rossetti," the genealogy stretching back to Johnson is most clearly visible:

> Let us begin with the biography—for what could be more amusing? As everybody knows, the fascination of reading biographies is irresistible. No sooner have we opened the pages of Miss Sandars's careful and competent book [*Life of Christina Rossetti*, by Mary F. Sandars (Hutchinson)] than the old illusion comes over us. Here is the past and all its inhabitants miraculously sealed as in a magic tank; all we have to do is to look and to listen and to listen and to look and soon the little figures—for they are rather under life size—will begin to move and to speak, and as they move we shall arrange them in all sorts of patterns of which they were ignorant, for they thought when they were alive that they could go where they liked; and as they speak we shall read into their sayings all kinds of meanings which never struck them, for they believed when they were alive that they said straight off whatever came into their heads. *But once you are in a biography all is different.*[6] (emphasis mine)

---

3. I owe a larger intellectual debt to this essay than particular acknowledgment can suggest.

4. Damrosch develops elements of this argument in *The Uses of Johnson's Criticism*, 135–48. Robert Folkenflik develops his version of this argument in *Samuel Johnson, Biographer*, 160–63. Martin Maner's *The Philosophical Biographer: Doubt and Dialectic in Johnson's Lives of the Poets* examines Johnson's biographical skepticism and his innovative rhetoric that combine doubt and dialectic into a distinctive way of knowing.

5. Wain, *Samuel Johnson*, 350; and Bate, *Samuel Johnson*, 531.

6. *Collected Essays*, 4:54.

Woolf and Johnson were fascinated by the same issues about writing other people's lives. Both believed that all biography is modern, since biographers cannot escape their points of view. Yet they also recognized their obligation responsibly to evoke the past. Both believed this responsibility to be related to, even conditioned by, another obligation. This obligation, as A. O. J. Cockshut, another of Johnson's heirs, has characterized it, is to "preserve the salutary humility of all good biography in the august presence of another soul."[7]

In a similar vein in the essay, "Lives of the Obscure," Woolf proposes her version of biographical thinking:

> For one likes romantically to feel oneself a deliverer advancing with lights across the waste of years to the rescue of some stranded ghost—a Mrs. Pilkington, a Rev. Henry Elman, a Mrs. Ann Gilbert—waiting, appealing, forgotten, in the growing gloom. Possibly they hear one coming. They shuffle, they preen, they bridle. Old secrets well up to their lips. The divine relief of communication will soon again be theirs. The dust shifts and Mrs. Gilbert—but the contact with life is instantly salutary. Whatever Mrs. Gilbert may be doing, she is not thinking about us.[8]

Reminiscent of Johnson's Preface to the *Dictionary*, Woolf begins by both imitating and correcting certain inflated notions of the biographer's task. The opening phrase, "For one likes romantically to feel oneself a deliverer," depicts the writer as heroine. The shift from the biographer's perspective to the subject's in the next sentence begins to revise the image of the biographer as someone quite different: "Possibly they hear one coming." Now the perspective shifts to the ghosts; it is they who are awaiting us. But the accent still falls on the biographer, who is being listened for and anxiously awaited: "Old secrets well up to their lips. The divine relief of communication will soon again be theirs." Now comes the contact with the biographer, which is for the ghost "instantly salutary." Then the reversal occurs as Woolf concludes: "Whatever Mrs. Gilbert may be doing, she is not thinking about us." Instantly we are humbled. It is not we as ourselves whom the ghost awaits. It is rather we as figures to speak with and through. The writer takes interest in the ghost in a manner and to a degree that never characterizes the ghost's interest in the biographer. Any biographer

---

7. *Truth to Life: The Art of Biography in the Nineteenth Century*, 20.
8. *Collected Essays*, 4:120.

worthy of the name, so Woolf believed, understands this crucial distinction and follows out its implications in her work.

Johnson's aside in the *Life of Edmund Smith* about Gilbert Walmsley, a friend and teacher from his early years, exhibits a similar awareness: "Of Gilbert Walmsley, thus presented to my mind, let me indulge myself in the remembrance. I knew him very early; he was one of the first friends that literature procured me, and I hope that at least my gratitude made me worthy of his notice" (LP 2:20). Such recollection may be, in part, the biographer's repaying a debt of gratitude. Gratitude is, as *Sermon* 15 defines it, a species of justice and thereby of truth. But it may also be a self-indulgence on the biographer's part. Johnson is conscious of this ambiguity and aware of its significance as a commentary on the poetics of biography. In particular, he is alert to the simple but important fact that it is the biographer who thinks about his or her subject, not the subject who thinks about the biographer.

Once stated, this observation may seem obvious. But both Johnson and Woolf thought the accent worth adding in order to emphasize an essential fact about the psychological condition in which biography develops. The writer's experience of thinking about, but not reciprocally being thought about, is surely as salutary for the biographer as is the ghost's opportunity to speak with the living. We may need from time to time, however, to be reminded of this therapeutic truth, since all the *thinking about* happens on our side.[9] This one-sidedness tends to distort our view. While Johnson does not pursue this insight in Woolf's manner or formulate it so explicitly, his work embodies the awareness pursued explicitly in hers. Thus she, in turn, helps us recover more of the force of his biographies by seeing its aftermath in her accomplishment.

SANITY AND GRATITUDE

To use Woolf's remarks as a way of focusing on Johnson's distinctive achievement in biography is to imitate Johnson himself. Throughout the *Lives* he acknowledges debts owed by one author to another and reminds us of the debts we owe to our intellectual forebears. He traces genealogies of education, sentiments, and technique. For him one of the ways sanity best displays itself is

9. In the essay "Virginia Woolf: The Biographer as Medium," I have developed aspects of this argument as they bear upon Woolf's poetics and practice of biography.

through acts of gratitude.[10] He records the names of the teachers of famous writers, notes who acknowledged debts and to whom, which sons rightly honored their parents, and who among parents lived long enough to enjoy their sons' successes. He understands such questions of indebtedness and inheritance to be more than simply matters of historical accuracy, although this would be important enough, or of some notion of proper accounting, although this, too, would not be negligible. Rather, these questions and his handling of them make possible writing about the past so that it becomes, not an unhappy, silencing burden but rather an empowering and consoling body of knowledge.[11] The past is for him neither a simple object of investigation nor an occasion for nostalgia.[12] It is the way human beings project themselves into the present, thence toward an imaginable and habitable future. To fail to mention the teachers of those writers to whom we, as readers, thereby also owe debts is to commit what Johnson calls in the *Life of Addison* a "historical fraud." Such fraud unpeoples the past, thus isolating us in the present unconnected with the past and future.

Johnson's high valuing of truth is a commonplace about his life and work. But it has particular philosophical and methodological significance when examined in the *Lives*, where he looks back over a lifetime of thinking about the various kinds of truths made available by imagining other people's lives. If by neglecting to name the teachers of those who have accomplished much we commit a historical fraud with serious implications for the erosion of present history and the denial of its future, conversely by naming them we do ourselves, even more than we do them, a service. By rehearsing our intellectual debts we bring the force of history creatively and powerfully to bear upon our present efforts.[13] To fail to grant, for instance, that, although Pope made errors of omission and commission in his edition of Shakespeare, he was still "the first that

10. Patricia Hampl expresses this interesting notion in her review, "Surviving a Life in the Present."

11. Vance in *Samuel Johnson and the Sense of History* discusses the way Johnson understands the use of history and particularly of feeling ourselves "as an extension of the past" to be the way of discovering "things that would last" and by that discovery to "feel reconciled to the inevitability of [our] own ends" (179, 178).

12. Friedrich Nietzsche proposes these ideas in *The Use and Abuse of History.*

13. Burke discusses this conception of inheritance in *Attitudes toward History*, 125.

knew, at least the first that told, by what helps the text might be improved" is a serious error. Such failure defrauds him of his "due praise" (LP 3:139). And such defrauding, while cheating Pope, is even more serious in the way it impoverishes our imaginations in at least two ways. By thus depriving ourselves of a clear view of our inheritance, we deny ourselves information necessary to define, undertake, and measure the success of our own projects. In failing to imagine how things might once have been other than they are now, we undermine normal, healthy receptivity to difference and thus damage our potential for creating something new.

In light of these issues it is interesting to consider once again Johnson's well-known critique of the metaphysical poets who, he observes, "never enquired what on any occasion they should have said or done, but wrote rather as beholders than partakers of human nature; as beings looking upon good and evil, impassive and at leisure; as Epicurean deities making remarks on the actions of men and the vicissitudes of life, without interest and without emotion" (LP 1:20). So, too, readers and critics make a similar mistake when they defraud past authors, or any to whom imaginative and intellectual debts are owed, of their due praise. In a similar vein he writes in the *Life of Addison:* "Before the profound observers of the present race repose too securely on the consciousness of their superiority to Addison, let them consider his *Remarks on Ovid*, in which may be found specimens of criticism sufficiently subtle and refined" (LP 2:148). The metaphysical poets and poor readers err alike in assuming a falsely elevated position relative to what they observe. Empathy and gratitude are expressions of sanity and accuracy.

To say this is not to blur the distinction between past and present or to mistake the meaning of past achievements. Shakespeare's plays, if written today, Johnson observes in his preface, would appear naive, perhaps even unacceptable and inadequate fictions. Similarly, Denham "improved our taste and advanced our language," yet still "left much to do" (LP 1:82). We do not now read his work, as did his contemporaries, to improve ourselves but rather to learn history, the better to appreciate what those who followed him accomplished. While not to read Thomas Sprat "with gratitude would only show our ignorance," both our gratitude and our ways of knowing him are almost surely different from the ways of his contemporaries, who read him for accounts of the newest scientific experiments and inquiries. Sprat's *History of the Royal*

Society is now read, Johnson observes, "not with the wish to know what they were then doing, but how their transactions are exhibited by Sprat" (LP 2:33). It is important to note different kinds of reading for the way their differences underscore the function of reading in the context of actual living. They also help explain how and why texts have different meanings over time. There is no single text, no single meaning to be discerned and preserved eternally.

There follows from this a corollary, namely that our inheritances, debts, and pleasures are interrelated. Accurately acknowledged pleasures, like accurately acknowledged debts, are an important individual and collective cultural resource. Chapter 2 discussed how an author like Shakespeare, who has pleased many and pleased long sufficiently to be called an ancient, becomes thereby a stable resource of pleasure and of truth, and hence a part of history on which future generations can rely. As one of his successive generations of readers, we may rely on him both for the substance of his work and for the line of inheritance to which the generations of his readers collectively belong. Hence the reason for Johnson's annoyance with critics who, led by mistaken notions about the worth of originality and fame, call into question Shakespeare's reputation. Such questioning is no longer legitimate; it is a kind of lie and thus carries with it the violence of the lie. This poet has passed beyond the need for justification, though he is not thereby beyond criticism. And precisely for this reason, to question his reputation is more harmful to us than to the poet. It is after all we, his heirs, who chiefly benefit from him and from the continuity of pleasure and truth embodied in his reputation, not he from us.

One can scarcely think of a critic less obsequious than Johnson, of one less unwilling to criticize where criticism is due, or of one more sensitive to the dangers of unconsidered praise. Yet he is equally sensitive to the real harm that results when readers fail rightly to recognize, as in the case of Shakespeare, how his reputation is an experimental, not an absolute, truth. The cumulative truth of his reputation, arrived at historically and probabilistically through many years and many readings, constitutes a conversation in the present between the present and the past. For a critic to interfere with Shakespeare's capacity to please threatens more than the poet's reputation or even the reader's pleasure, although this latter is for Johnson no small threat. Instead it threatens more largely the very ground of human communication. Such a notion of the promise and legitimacy of a present that is substantially related to the past serves for Johnson as a healthful preventative of the grave errors in thinking that inevitably occur when we unpeople the past. Notable among these errors are the fantasies of omnipotence that usually result in dull thinking, loneliness, and the histrionics of self-destructive melancholy. To inspire good thinking our histories must be excessively crowded, our gratitude energetic and varied. Johnson does not narrowly measure the implications of omitting thanks. Gratitude is one crucial aspect of imagining a present and earning our inheritance by perceiving that inheritance to be the foundation of a new project or problem to be made distinctively our own.

To fail to acknowledge debts is then not merely a social or even just a moral failure but rather more encompassingly an epistemological error and a sin against pleasure. To fail to live in the midst of a many-voiced conversation with the past in the present results in lives lived like the miserable inhabitants of the happy valley who are bored and bitter because they refuse to imagine indebtedness and to recognize difference. Biography offers precisely the necessary exercise in imaginative excess and the recognition of difference to counteract such dangers because, by imagining others, we empower ourselves to use the present well. Such empowerment is the aim of one of the historical exercises proposed by Johnson in the *Life of Dryden*. He notes how difficult it is to imagine the state of English criticism before Dryden wrote his *Essay of Dramatick Poesie*, a work whose assumptions so shaped subsequent thinking about literature that we can scarcely imagine a time before they were in the air. Not to give this critic his due is an instance of a kind of epistemological autism that denies us our full powers of mind. By acknowledging in detail and actively thinking through our inheritance from those like Dryden who changed a culture's manner of thinking we prepare ourselves to undertake our own projects in the present. This is the chief use of biography.

While the theme of *Rasselas* is the importance, difficulties, and rewards of keeping a conversation going among different people, the theme of the *Lives of the Poets* is the use and pleasure of the many-voiced drama of reading that constitutes literary history—a drama in which we may differ from one another and even from ourselves over time. Recognizing that all of his readers may not, for instance, be equally interested in the cancels of Pope's *Iliad*, Johnson ends his catalog of examples before he personally might wish to stop. Pope's cancels may fascinate professional writers, but Johnson is not writing to writers only. He admits that he, as critic, is sometimes bored or forgetful and that he sometimes fails to finish what he has begun. Throughout he emphasizes that his readers' first responsibility is to the author in question, not to the critic-biographer. Ultimately he endorses the reader's right to differ with him. The perception and valuing of difference, whether it be the capacity to imagine a time before Dryden had established the first principles of English criticism, or the possibility that all readers may not find Pope's cancels equally fascinating, figure centrally in Johnson's canon of critical principles. They are an exercise in culti-vating the kind of alertness that makes education not an activity narrowly and mistakenly relegated to our early years but the habit of a lifetime.

The *Lives* call forth from readers a kind of attention equated by Johnson with learning, as he brings into focus aspects of these writ-ers' work, lives, creative intelligence, and reception often border-ing on invisibility. Consider, for instance, his reference to two fig-ures in the *Life of Savage*. There is the jailer, a man whose kindness in circumstances of conventional brutality and hardheartedness make him the prototype of inventive goodness. Johnson thinks this man deserving of special note. There is also Savage's unnamed woman relative who similarly deserves mention because of her kindness to him "in opposition to influence, precept, and example" (LP 2:337). Or consider Richard Steele, on the subject of whose remarkable love for his more gifted friend Addison, Johnson com-ments: "It is not hard to love those from whom nothing can be feared, and Addison never considered Steele as a rival; but Steele lived, as he confesses, under an habitual subjection to the predom-inating genius of Addison, whom he always mentioned with rever-ence and treated with obsequiousness" (LP 2:81). The passage iden-tifies how loving another person more talented than oneself gives evidence of the way a generous imagination can invent emotional possibilities beyond narrow self-interest or envy. Steele's friend-ship with Addison is a model of generous invention avoiding the more common reactions of jealousy and estrangement. Like Dry-den's revolutionizing intelligence in the *Essay of Dramatick Poesie*, Steele's uncommon creativity gives evidence of a kind of genius that can never be predicted. The *Lives* cumulatively instruct the reader in a readiness to recognize such acts of genius wherever they may occur and thus to mock-encounter with the possibility of per-forming them ourselves.

Such readiness is a projection of the capacity to perceive and to think in ways other than those already familiar. This readiness bears significantly upon the act of criticism, in particular upon the relation between reason and emotion in the critical act. In the *Life of Pope* Johnson acknowledges his preference for Dryden over Pope in a manner that invites testing over time: "If the reader should suspect me, as I suspect myself, of some partial fondness for the memory of Dryden, let him not too hastily condemn me; for meditation and enquiry may, perhaps, shew him the reasonableness of my determination" (LP 3:223). The oxymoron juxtaposing the critic's "reasonableness" and his "partial fondness" expresses a characteristically Johnsonian truth about the nature of literature and literary judgments.[14] Critical judgments about literature do not originate from critical principles, although they may be guided by these principles. Rather they depend on experience and comparison. No explicit rules exist for making discoveries or for formulating more adequate conceptions from our experience.[15] Although criticism is, from Johnson's point of view, subordinate to literature, it is not thereby different in kind. The fact that in both literature and criticism "judgement is always in some degree subject to affection" (LP 2:47) is no more a liability to one of these pursuits than to the other. Yet it does equally challenge both.

HOW WAS THE WORK PERFORMED?

In the *Life of Dryden* Johnson attempts to imagine from the evidence of the writing the qualities of Dryden's mind:

> A mind like Dryden's, always curious, always active, to which every understanding was proud to be associated, and of which every one solicited the regard by an ambitious display of himself, had a more pleasant, perhaps a nearer, way to knowledge than by the silent progress of solitary reading. I do not suppose that he despised books or intentionally neglected them; but that he was carried out by the impetuosity of his genius to more vivid and speedy instructors, and that his studies were rather desultory and fortuitous than constant and systematical. . . . Of all this however if the proof be demanded I will not undertake to give it; *the atoms of probability, of which my opinion has*

14. Clarence Tracy comments in the introduction to his edition of the *Life of Savage* that "as a biographer Johnson never had Boswell's eager curiosity for facts, and relied more than Boswell did on his own insights" and that the "characteristic tone [of the *Lives of the Poets*] is that of judicial appraisal" (xiii, xvii).

15. Polanyi elaborates this notion about there being no "rules" for making discoveries or improving our conceptions (*Personal Knowledge*, 52).

been formed, lie scattered over all his works: and by him who thinks
the question worth his notice his works must be perused with very
close attention. (LP 1:417, 418; emphasis mine)

Johnson's metaphor for the constitutive elements of his critical
opinion figures forth one of the beliefs in things invisible recurrent
in the *Lives:* a trust in thinking, as opposed to mere thought,
which, as *Rasselas* examines fictionally, is chiefly characterized by
a healthy attitude toward difference.

This attitude is epitomized in the anecdote, earlier noted, of
Johnson's reply to the friend who asked if he thought he had sometimes too brutally contradicted people: "What harm does it do to
any man," Johnson rebuked his friend, "to be contradicted?" For
him such contradiction is one of our chief ways of knowing. Like
the common spark of genius that illuminates the past and shadows
forth an imagined future, contradiction is crucial to survival. Along
the lines of James Sutherland's comment that the emphasis on reason in the eighteenth century indicates precisely that the concept
was not then taken for granted, one might observe that for Johnson,
as well, contradiction, or the healthy acting out of difference, was so
crucial for living that it, too, could not be taken for granted. A sensitivity to difference accounts for our recognizing such important
truths as the fact that something "which is easy at one time was
difficult at another" (LP 1:411). It helps us to understand that all
things are not equally easy or difficult for everyone or even for any
single individual at different times. These insights, while simple
enough conceptually, often prove difficult to apply practically because they require not so much perseverance and intelligence as patience and an impersonal confidence about our place in history.

The foregoing relate collectively to one of Johnson's chief interests in writing the *Lives,* an interest in satisfying his own and subsequently the reader's curiosity about how writing is written:
"When any work has been viewed and admired the first question of
intelligent curiosity is, how was it performed?" (LP 1:213). To ask
this question gives evidence of a mind that can imagine things as
other than they are now and a time before the work was performed.
Such imagining, in turn, conditions the possibility for inquiry into
the past and movement into the future. There is the time before
something is done and the time after. The activity occurring in the
interval must always be invented. It never simply happens. Even an
ordinary thought or action has its wonderful aspects because, as
Johnson recognized, there always exists the other possibility of

nothing being done. No action or thought is inevitable. Things do not have to happen as they happened, although the grammar of facts carries a bewitching aura of necessity. Precisely for this reason, so the *Lives* cumulatively remind us, the reader must struggle against this bewitchment by engaging in accurate historical thinking that imagines free will, circumstance, and chance all operating in the lives of our predecessors.

Considering the temporal quality of writing (the fact that its composition history has a before and an after and that our reading, too, unfolds in time) is also an exercise in imagining the mind of the author in time as that mind made something that once did not exist and now does. Such imagining also identifies the element of creativity central to Johnson's sense of the energy and interest of life. To be sure, he takes special interest in unusually gifted and energetic writers. The creative activity of Pope and Dryden engages him in more elaborate imaginings of how their work was performed than, say, Pomfret's. But throughout the *Lives* a refrain of democratic interest in the origins and phenomena of creativity sounds. From this refrain the reader becomes increasingly aware of the force of a culture's literary inheritance being a record of activity, not merely a catalog of accomplishments. Johnson's primary questions about a piece of writing (Why did it come about? And how was it performed?) are designed to engage and to shape into narrative the imaginative possibility of human freedom. These questions and the answers they evoke rescue authors from the past and from the seeming inevitability of their accomplishments if viewed only retrospectively. His questions save these authors from the fate they often suffer at the hands of unimaginative readers, of seeming always to have known exactly what they were going to do, how they were going to do it, and why.

Devotion to work manifests the general yearning for immortality. Although not a recantation of the ethos of *The Vanity of Human Wishes*, the *Lives* do take a markedly different perspective on the question of what one can, without vanity, ultimately hope for. In the *Life of Butler* where Johnson asks the question that drives his inquiry into all the writers' lives, "How was the work performed?" his answer focuses on the belief in things invisible. This belief also underwrites the model of creativity in the *Lives*:

> *Hudibras* was not a hasty effusion; it was not produced by a sudden tumult of imagination, or a short paroxysm of violent labour. To accumulate such a mass of sentiments at the call of accidental desire or of

sudden necessity is beyond the reach and power of the most active and comprehensive mind. I am informed by Mr. Thyer of Manchester, the excellent editor of this author's reliques, that he could shew something like *Hudibras* in prose. He has in his possession the commonplace book, in which Butler reposited, not such events or precepts as are gathered by reading; but such remarks, similitudes, allusions, assemblages, or inferences as occasion prompted or meditation produced; those thoughts that were generated in his own mind, and might be usefully applied to some future purpose. Such is the labour of those who write for immortality. (LP 1:213)

Using both the work and evidence about Butler's commonplace book, Johnson tries to imagine how this writer went about his work, defined questions, gathered and recorded thoughts "that might be usefully applied to some future purpose." Such activity can, at the outset, be imagined only generally and thus must be guided by trust in some future aim that becomes clear only after it is accomplished.

Although he believes in the virtues of hard work, Johnson is not narrowly or literally devoted to work for its own sake. He believes in what persevering effort signifies. If not precisely the earthly equivalent of immortality, it is at least a force contributing to make the past imaginatively real by embodying purpose and example. Even the metaphysical poets, whom Johnson criticized for their unpoetic poetry, earned his praise for their hard work: "No man could be born a metaphysical poet" (LP 1:21). This imagined reality of the past is itself a crucial resource of meaning and energy for our efforts in the present and future. Human wishes are vain if they limit their criteria of satisfaction to the single aim of achieving permanence of the work or even permanent effects. But they are not vain if they refocus their perspective to include the intent, preparation, and energy that went into the work.

The Vanity of Human Wishes offers another insight into the issues so far discussed in this chapter. It is a young man's poem of grand resignation and dramatic humility.[16] In order to critique the

---

16. In his essay, "Johnson and *The Life of Savage*," William Vesterman comments on the strong sense of "personal involvement" everywhere present in *The Vanity of Human Wishes* by contrast with the earlier poem *London*. He speculates that in writing the *Life of Savage* Johnson learned how to invest himself in his writing of biography. In a related vein Carmen J. Pomponio's essay, "Looking at Johnson's *Life of Dryden*," identifies the driving force of this life to be its "openness, the authentic attitude of enquiry, the persistent probing into the question of biography, the question of John Dryden" (37).

mistaken hope that wishing can be satisfied by particular objects, the poet hypostatizes the effects of the "anxious toil" and "eager strife" that men and women eagerly perform. This is not to say that the poet and his speaker make the same mistake identified by the poem but rather to note that correction cannot occur completely outside the system of error it identifies. The author's emphasis must fall in the manner of the mistake itself. By contrast, the ethos of the *Lives* is at once humbler and more mature. By the end of his life Johnson had come to understand creativity to be a kind of earthly immortality, not in its effects or its causes but in the very fact of its occurrence. Its occurrence, he believed by inference, also figures forth the promise of something beyond mere human accomplishment, something that accomplishment ultimately stands for.

The passage from the *Life of Butler* continues with a warning repeated throughout the *Lives*: "But human works are not easily found without a perishable part." Johnson elaborates this observation in a passage well worth citing in full as an example of his distinctive insight into the simultaneous challenge and resource of attempting to imagine the past:

> Of the ancient poets every reader feels the mythology tedious and oppressive. Of *Hudibras* the manners, being founded on opinions, are temporary and local, and therefore become every day less intelligible and less striking. What Cicero says of philosophy is true likewise of wit and humour, that 'time effaces the fictions of opinion, and confirms the determinations of Nature.' Such manners as depend upon standing relations and general passions are co-extended with the race of man; but those modifications of life and peculiarities of practice which are the progeny of error and perverseness, or at best of some accidental influence or transient persuasion, must perish with their parents.
>
> Much therefore of that humour which transported the last century with merriment is lost to us, who do not know the sour solemnity, the sullen superstition, the gloomy moroseness, and the stubborn scruples of the ancient Puritans; or if we know them, derive our information only from books or from tradition, have never had them before our eyes, and cannot but by recollection and study understand the lines in which they are satirised. Our grandfathers knew the picture from the life; we judge of the life by contemplating the picture. (LP 1:213–14)

The moment when the reversal of the primary interpretative elements of literature (*life* and the *picture* of that life) occurs is the moment marking the divide between past and present. As long as the pictures of literature are known from life, the work is contemporary. But when the life can be understood only from the picture, the work has become part of the past. What then is missing from the experience of reading is life itself. The reader's acquaintance with that life can no longer be assumed as part of the equipment for reading. The reversal of interpretative elements evident in the preceding passage has profound implications for reading—for the expectations and methods brought by readers to this activity, for the kinds of acquaintance and recognition, understanding, and pleasure they typically expect. When a work is no longer our contemporary, we often mistake its historical differences for errors rather than identifying them as discontinuities between the work's contemporary context and our own. Johnson astutely identifies this mistake.

Earlier I mentioned that the *Lives* as a whole assert that the chief qualification for reading is sensitivity to how "that which is easy at one time was difficult at another" (LP 1:411). Johnson analyzes literary history and the history of reading as he approaches all human achievement, which is to say as a history of problems solved. All authors solve problems, but some solve harder and more interesting problems than others, and some accomplish what has never before been done. Such achievement is difficult to measure in its own time because to measure it by current standards is to assess it in terms of what it is not. If the achievement alters how the majority of people think and act, it may be equally difficult to measure later because by then it has become too familiar and natural even to recognize.

The difficulty encountered in attempting to read works of genius from the past recapitulates the challenge originally encountered by the creator of that work. In a manner resembling his observation in the *Journey* about second sight being located along a continuum of the ordinary operations of the mind, Johnson conceives of the imaginative leap of genius that does things differently from the way they are done now as being perceptible only by a like activity of mind. He notes a famous instance of such failure in an anecdote about Addison and the young Pope. Pope consulted Addison about whether or not to expand his early two-canto version of *The Rape of the Lock*. Addison advised him not to. Of this advice, notoriously suspect in light of the magnificent poem that Pope eventually wrote, Johnson observes:

> This has been too hastily considered as an instance of Addison's jealousy; for as he could not guess the conduct of the new design, or the possibilities of pleasure comprised in a fiction of which there had been

no examples, he might very reasonably and kindly persuade the author to acquiesce in his own prosperity, and forbear an attempt which he considered as an unnecessary hazard. (LP 3:103)

He begins by addressing the question of Addison's motive, pointing out how, if the question is superficially considered, Addison may appear to be, at worst, envious, at best, self-interested. Construing the evidence in this way is certainly uncharitable. Given Johnson's equation among gratitude, justice, and sanity, uncharitableness such as this is no small failing. But it is unsatisfactory for other reasons as well. This uncharitable construction is also less probable than one that posits a more common failing, if *failing* is even the right word. Addison could neither imagine what Pope was capable of doing (How could he?) nor imagine the possibilities of pleasure available from a new species of fiction. He therefore plausibly advised the young writer to leave well enough alone and "to acquiesce in his own prosperity." With this phrase Johnson introduces the reader into Pope's imagination. Even as a young writer he was self-confident. He knew neither complacency nor fear. This drama of self-confidence finding ways to project its energy into the world was for Johnson the origin of all great accomplishment. Inquiring after it was for him the chief interest of biography.

Addison's motive was probably neither envy to subdue a young contender nor a misplaced emphasis on the material rewards of safe success. It is both more probable and more charitable to assume that he was simply incapable of fully imagining the young man's original talent and self-confidence. Addison failed his young friend because he could not imagine things from his point of view. He failed to "foresee the future efflorescence of imagery then budding in his mind" and was unable to imagine the kind of dedication to "spare no art or industry of cultivation" (LP 3:103) that characterized this genius. Addison failed Pope as a teacher by failing to know him well enough—a failure that Johnson saw at the heart of all mistakes in education. Yet while the older man's mistake became visible only in retrospect, it nonetheless materially threatened the very possibility of genius unfolding in its own present. While it is difficult to fault Addison who, like the Scots historian Martin, could hardly have known what he did not know, it is equally difficult to forgive him. Still, his advice also served paradoxically as the occasion for true genius, a force grounded in self-confidence and prescient of its future, to challenge, test, and perhaps even inspire itself.

DIFFICULTY

Sanity and gratitude intersect in the realm of history as we attempt to consider the past as a set of problems encountered and defined, solutions imagined and undertaken. Discerning these difficulties requires an imaginative reconstruction of the context of the work. Reconstructing difficulties encountered and solved was, for Johnson, the principal interest of history and hence the chief task of the historian. Related to this understanding was his exasperation with authors who announce that they had no difficulties in their work. Ease, he thought, is inevitably feigned. He believed this less because he valued work for its own sake than because he perceived a simple logic in the relation between difficulty and praise. "Where there is no difficulty there is no praise," he observes in the *Life of Dryden* (LP 1:339). No one can honestly think otherwise, although many behave as if they do.

Along similar lines in the *Life of Congreve* he criticizes his "strange affectation" all too frequent in authors "of appearing to have done every thing by chance" (LP 2:214). He recounts Voltaire's disgust at Congreve's "despicable foppery of desiring to be considered not as an author but a gentleman; to which the Frenchman replied, 'that if he had been only a gentleman, he should not have come to visit him'" (LP 2:226). If there were no difficulty, there would be no grounds to claim fame or praise for having succeeded in one's work. Success is a term defined in relation to the challenge of the work undertaken. Congreve's affectation forbids his making any claims upon our praise for the work accomplished or our interest in the difficulties of its creation. Difficulty is a quality historical and relative; it is not an absolute. It thereby follows that difficulty has a history. What was difficult at one time may not be difficult at another. Hence the frequent invisibility of past achievements. Hence, too, the usefulness of writing a history of difficulty, which might be given as the subtitle to the *Lives*.

If difficulty evokes in the genius a belief in things invisible that we call confidence, in the reader something analogous must be evoked. Reading also requires confidence. The readers must in some sense feel secure in the present and thus confident to attempt imagining difference in the past. Confidence is for Johnson the chief characteristic of great writers.[17] It is the form assumed by

17. Folkenflik takes this tack on confidence by developing the notion of the writer as hero in *Samuel Johnson, Biographer.*

their heroism. He is quick to admit that heroes have their liabilities and that those who are not heroes are often more appealing generally as people and specifically as acquaintances and friends:

> Gay is represented as a man easily incited to hope, and deeply depressed when his hopes were disappointed. This is not the character of a hero; but it may naturally imply something more generally welcome, a soft and civil companion. Whoever is apt to hope good from others is diligent to please them; but he that believes his powers strong enough to force their own way, commonly tries only to please himself. (LP 2:272)

The distinction asserted in this passage is a crucial one whose significance Johnson had learned over the years. Sensitive to the decent civilities and pleasures of companionship and familiar with the hardships of doing without them, he never undervalued them. But neither did he undervalue the importance of heroes who speak and act eccentrically, outside the circle of companionship and precedent.

He also knew that, even if we could successfully repress heroes, we could not really get along without them for they embody the force of self-confidence, "the first requisite of great undertakings" (LP 3:89). Whether like Milton or Dryden, who succeeded despite the difficulty inherent in their ambitious projects, or like Pope, tested by the subtler and more tempting dangers of a well-meaning friend's discouragement, such creators will not be deterred. In each instance, the writer is driven by more than the force of ego, a force partaking equally of desire that moves outward into production and self-absorption that moves inward for protection. This different force is evident in the case of Blackmore, for whom writing was "his transcendent pleasure, and as he was not deterred by censure, he was not satiated with praise" (LP 2:244). The energy of such writers comes from elsewhere. They are, at least sometimes in their lives, independent of the pull of custom and society. All good writers must to some degree achieve their independence. Some, like Denham, achieve it in stages, so that examining his versification "will afford that pleasure which arises from the observation of a man of judgement naturally right forsaking bad copies by degrees and advancing towards a better practice, as he gains more confidence in himself" (LP 1:80). While Denham developed his confidence over time, some writers seem from the outset to be gifted with a confidence directing them for life.

Milton and Pope are Johnson's foremost examples of this kind of confidence that inspired their remarkable work, although it also disabled them in certain ways. Johnson analyzes the allied gains and losses of Milton's genius by remarking: "It appears in all his writings that he had the usual concomitant of great abilities, a lofty and steady confidence in himself, perhaps not without some contempt of others; for scarcely any man ever wrote so much and praised so few" (LP 1:94). The other side of the poet's confidence in himself was his sparing praise of others.[18] So, too, for Pope his genius both enabled and disabled him: "Not knowing how to use what was not his own," Johnson remarks, "he spoiled the thought when he had borrowed it" (LP 2:129). Here Johnson acutely perceives another pair of linked assets and liabilities in the mind of genius. Pope was constitutionally incapable of successfully borrowing from other writers. Other lesser writers may borrow with beauty and success, but not the genius, whose disability is identical with his gift. Pope's greatest asset and liability came from the same creative source. His genius was to know how to enact his creativity with rather than against its natural inclination and to direct his talents in such way that the materials he chose would successfully take the imprint of his energies as if nature itself had made the mark.

CONFIDENCE IN LEARNING

Looking back over Johnson's career from the vantage point of the *Lives*, we can recognize with greater force and precision the significance of his lifelong commitment to education combined with his anxiety and skepticism regarding how much or even if we can realistically hope to educate one another and ourselves. He saw many impediments. Fear of difference, boredom, and the failure of curiosity constantly threaten learning. Even the seemingly positive virtues of respect for past achievements and enjoyment of our own work tempt us not to complete an undertaking.

The *Lives of the Poets* embodies a different educational ethos and offers a different perspective on the question of what we may hope for and from education. A letter from Becker to his friend Louis Gottschalk, mentioned earlier, aptly identifies Johnson's

---

18. On the related subject of Johnson's emphasis on bringing into view and examining the question of whether there are grounds for the praise given to an author in order to "reassess received opinions and exert influence" see Mark W. Booth, "Johnson's Critical Judgments in the *Lives of the Poets.*"

agenda with its emphasis on the interconnected problem and necessity of discerning past achievements:

> I like particularly your emphasis on the fact that we can't count on
> people *not learning* from experience. . . . Hence you may say that any
> theory about the behavior of man in the past, in so far as men accept it
> and act on it, falsifies the theory because it introduces a new condition
> into the factors that determine the behavior of men in the future. . . .
> If Marx wanted his theory to remain valid (supposing it was valid for
> the past) for the future, he should have kept it to himself. I have ex-
> pressed this difference by saying that "fortunately for the physicist the
> atom cannot acquire a knowledge of physics."[19]

Becker analyzes the problems that plague those who attempt to
construct theories of human behavior—problems arising from the
fact that the objects of such theory are also the thinking subjects.
Thinking about human behavior often changes human behavior.
By the time Johnson came to write the *Lives*, he had arrived at a
similar insight; namely that if you can't count on people to learn,
neither can you count on their not learning. And this learning, so
Dryden, too, discovered, alters history. Having invented and popu-
larized the critical preface, he "found his readers made suddenly
too skilful to be easily satisfied" (LP 1:366).

In order for discernment and learning to thrive, readers and writers alike must be willing to accept mental irritants, to recognize
and even to enjoy this irony of successful education, as in the case
of Dryden's experience of the pressure that his success put on his
subsequent efforts. His success in inventing the critical preface
made more work for him, to be sure. But it also made more work for
his readers because they found themselves now, in requiring more
of him, also requiring more of themselves. Only by accepting such
commitments to live up to the effects of successful teaching can we
see the past and learn well enough in the present not to be too
easily satisfied with past achievements and specious pleasures. To
fail in this undertaking is to risk the fate of the inhabitants of the
happy valley, who settle miserably for inadequate notions of pleasure. They fail fully to imagine and live out the consequences of
genuine creativity. They fail to see the artifacts of culture, their
relations with one another, their hopes, successes, and failures as
the starting place for a distinctive kind of imaginative inquiry. The
aim of such inquiry is knowledge by acquaintance. Its aim is to

---

19. *"What is the Good of History?,"* 320, 321.

weave a new design of intelligibility and purpose into the fabric of present action.

In his typically Johnsonian manner Burke proposes hypnosis as a figure for the way we learn by analogy, forming our response to new situations on the basis of what we have learned from the past and thus integrating past and present.[20] Given this understanding of how we learn, he continues, "it would seem to follow that we must, to an extent, be hypnotized by a past situation while confronting a new one." But there is good hypnosis and bad hypnosis, and the two must be distinguished. The difference lies in understanding that learning from past experience presumes a present need. Thought and its application cannot, Johnson knew, be separated. This insight accounts for his investment in the reality of his own and other people's lives as the philosophical, emotional, and moral ground of his thinking.

These combined aspects of his thought were identified by Lytton Strachey, himself a revolutionary biographical thinker, who called these qualities Johnson's "searching sense of actuality." In other words, Johnson went one step beyond Hume in his emphasis on saving the appearances by truly taking them at face value. The actual for Johnson does not go without saying, nor is seeing itself a given. While our cultural heritage is a resource on which we can rely, its value lies precisely in its being the sum of everything about which we may be totally mistaken.[21] Not to recognize and live with and by this understanding is to risk becoming alienated from our inheritance. There is no state of leisure. We must perennially earn our past. Just as it is foolish to claim success while at the same time claiming that no difficulty has been encountered, so it is equally foolish to claim importance for something that would make no difference if we were to get it badly wrong. If we wish to claim the former possibility, then we must also be willing to claim and to accept the implications of the latter. Hence the need for a continual, active conversation with our imagined past and future. So, too, for relations with people, both living and dead. Their value exists not despite, but because of, the possibility of their going wrong.

While Johnson's primary orientation in the world involved fierce doubting, it was not for nothing that he loved what he in-

20. "The Relation between Literature and Science."
21. Polanyi, *Personal Knowledge*, 404.

ferred from the minds of such creators as Milton and Dryden to be the chief qualities of their minds: an adventurous, sometimes heedless, bounding energy, confidence, and belief in their work. It was precisely because he loved such imaginative restlessness that he recognized the need for the kind of active, searching, passionate inquiry and conversation that this study has tracked throughout his career.[22] Our ways and means of knowing express and embody us, and yet also press beyond into what Polanyi has described as "the emergent noosphere," which is to say "the external pole of our commitments, the service of which is our freedom."[23] Beginning in his early years and with increasing precision and passion along the way, Johnson believed that knowledge enters the world personally and dramatically, becoming truly ours only as we think through our own and other people's lives.

22. "Imaginative restlessness" is Knoblauch's phrase in the essay "Coherence Betrayed" (250) to describe the quality of mind that Johnson so prizes in Milton and Dryden. For a related approach to Johnson and biography, see Stephen J. Fix, "Distant Genius: Johnson and the Art of Milton's Life," where he discusses the way Johnson "actively sought to connect Milton's life and art" (245); and "Johnson and the 'Duty' of Reading *Paradise Lost*."

23. *Personal Knowledge*, 404.

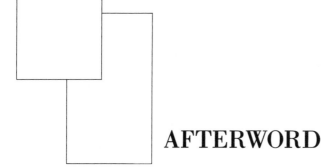

AFTERWORD

Among Johnson's chief strengths as a writer, so I have argued, are his insights into how people think and his skill in characterizing their ways of thinking. Both his own mind and those of other people fascinated him. He enjoyed imagining how we think. He also believed such imagining to be of real, practical use morally, ethically, and aesthetically for writers and readers alike. In his *Preface to Shakespeare*, for instance, he praises the poet for having "a vigilance of observation and accuracy of distinction which books and precepts cannot confer" and from which "almost all original and native excellence proceeds" (YJ 7:88). Of Richard Savage he remarked that "he had the art of escaping from his own reflections, and accommodating himself to every new scene" (LP 2:430). Savage thus lived a life rich with the possibility for self-instruction. More the pity, his friend observes, that he squandered it. Such instances of Johnson's biographical insight are the outcroppings of a distinctive habit of mind, drawn by temperament and application to imagine other minds and in so doing to contemplate his own.

A person's characteristic ways of thinking were for him something very like the life force itself.[1] Hence his interest in them. How the subject in question thought was Johnson's first and foremost curiosity and concern in any inquiry. Furthermore, he understood this to be a common interest, one that the biographer's work may epitomize but by no means uniquely embodies or exhausts. This perception is the origin of my study's attempt to describe

---

1. Lipking remarks on our avoidance of the term *meaning of life* and of discussing this concept in Johnson's work in his notable essay "Johnson and the Meaning of Life."

Johnson's profoundly biographical habits of thought as these habits, in turn, informed his thinking generally and served as his perspective on all things. Seeing how these notions underwrite his work by examining representative instances of his fiction, essays, travel writing, and biography has been the chief motive and aim of my undertaking. Biography as a genre was, to be sure, important to Johnson; he often wrote it. But as I have emphasized, biography was for him more than merely a literary form. He understood it to be mode of understanding and living in the world. Here lies its chief interest for us. Beyond this aim relevant to Johnson and his work, my study also makes a case for how, by example, he empowers us to enlarge the place and function of biography in our lives.

It is also evident from his life and work that he did not consider thinking to be a narrowly intellectual or merely cognitive activity. For him mind and life were in some fundamental sense synonymous. Thinking is life and life, thinking. We are familiar with instances of this belief as, for example, the anecdote about how he tested his faculties after a stroke by composing a Latin poem. This incident suggests dramaturgically his belief in thinking as a vital principle. His sense of what thinking was withstood the modern temptation to divide life (soma) from mind or soul (psyche).[2] He was critical, even contemptuous of those who, like the French savants, used "the mere power of their own minds," finding in this mistaken epistemology the explanation of their having "little power." Johnson did not locate thinking in the mind alone.[3]

In light of the foregoing, it would not seem farfetched to call Johnson's thinking psychosomatic, as well as to call his vocation of writing, considered from the perspective of its motives and ultimate aims, bio-graphy, also in its root meaning of life writing. These terms identify qualities of his mind evident in his life and, in turn, experienced by readers in his work. They also focus on the particular ways his work has claimed readers' attention over the

2. DeMaria in Johnson's Dictionary discusses "Johnson's unwillingness to give up a connection between mind and soul" (92–95). Rhodes in " 'Idler' No. 24 and Johnson's Epistemology" makes the following suggestive observation: "To Johnson, who defined energy in his Dictionary as 'life,' the mind thinking afforded conclusive evidence that man's dependence on matter guarantees his independence and a final proof that man's loss of intellectual stature but qualifies him the more to obtain it" (21). And Bate in Achievement of Samuel Johnson observes "that the mind is an activity" (95).

3. Cited in Jeffrey Hart, "Some Thoughts on Johnson as Hero," 33.

years.[4] Finally, they reanimate the force of his ideas and beliefs about the relationship between literature and life, thinking and living.[5] The virtues of such terms are, in other words, more than merely taxonomic. They contribute toward establishing and pursuing a new emphasis in Johnson studies, one that, while it returns to the nineteenth-century interest in the man himself, returns with a difference determined by the twentieth-century emphasis on his writing.

The force that the drama of thinking carried in his life is often measured with reference jointly to his argumentative instincts and to the pleasure he took in talking for victory. Such measurement is not inaccurate, but it is misleadingly narrow. When asked if he did not sometimes think he had been too hard on his opponents, he responded with puzzlement and genuine surprise. He could not understand people, or at least refused to admit to understanding them, whose feelings were hurt by honest argument, because he understood energetic disagreement to be a crucial aspect of living, a sign of being fully alive. Johnson condescended to no man's, woman's, or child's mind. He advised Mrs. Thrale on educating her young children that babies do not want to hear about babies but about giants, castles, and other subjects that stretch and stimulate their minds. He took other people's minds, at whatever age, as seriously as he took his own, considering them to be our greatest resource of pleasure and surprise, as well as evidence of the inter-animation of the rational and the empirical in our earthly lives.

Boswell characterized Johnson's superiority as consisting "chiefly in what may be called the art of thinking, the art of using his mind; a certain continual power of seizing the useful substance of all that he knew, and exhibiting it in a clear and forcible manner; so that knowledge, which we often see to be no better than lumber in men of dull understanding, was, in him, true, evident, and actual wisdom."[6] Johnson is chiefly valued for having such a mind—a mind that believed that thinking, like life itself, precisely by virtue of its limitations, gives evidence from which the infinite and the immaterial may be inferred. Because he holds such beliefs about

4. Two essays of particular interest on the subject of the interrelationship between literature and life in Johnson's writing are Watt's "Dr. Johnson and the Literature of Experience" and Lipking's "Johnson and the Meaning of Life."

5. William R. Keast proposes this notion of criticism as recovery in "Johnson's Criticism of the Metaphysical Poets," 302.

6. Boswell, *Life*, 4:427–28.

mind and thinks accordingly, more than perhaps for any other single reason, reading Johnson must be the activity of a lifetime, though we probably make the discovery the other way around: Reading him over a lifetime, we discover that he has such a mind. We piece him together over time as we learn through him to identify within ourselves and others the art of thinking for which we ultimately recognize some indebtedness to him. It is an art of thinking occurring not merely in the mind, neither in his nor in our own, but rather through him in us. My study has taken this understanding of the man as the fundamental cue for its method and aims.

Thus, while Johnson's thinking is challenging and often novel, it never seems unfamiliar or, in the conventional sense of the word, difficult. He never asks of his readers more than he believes they, at their best, would ask of themselves. He never proposes thoughts or questions that curious readers who take the time and have the courage could not formulate on their own, though not without differences one from another. His writing is deeply motivated by this principle of efficiency. Believing that we should share with one another what we do best, he simply offers his own best. Thus it is no accident that one of his particular talents was to draw people out on subjects they knew well, could speak confidently on, and could thereby inform others about effectively.

In *The Dying Self*, mentioned earlier in this study, the author observes that genuinely good people are characterized by the way their powers seem always to be available to them. They make goodness seem, if not precisely easy, at least efficient, sensible, and desirable. They demonstrate how goodness is not a complex or difficult responsibility but generally the simplest and most satisfactory course to pursue. We experience such people, Fair observes, as psychosomatically organized.[7] This definition of organization as a practical ideal is characteristically Johnsonian in the way it combines ethics and psychology. Like Aristotle's notion of the *habitus* ("an inner quality or stable and deep-rooted disposition that raises the human subject and his natural powers to a higher degree of vital formation and energy"), such organization also gives evidence of our educability.[8] To be organized in this sense does not mean simply being orderly, but it does mean understanding the dangerous and inevitable consequences of being disorganized. Evil, as John-

---

7. Fair, *Dying Self*, 202.
8. Jacques Maritain, "Art as a Virtue of the Practical Intellect," 48–49.

son understood its habitual operations, takes root in disorganization. By contrast, organization is the phenomenon, the appearance, of morality. Such interest and concerns are, in turn, at the heart of the way he "thought biography."

Let me illustrate from my own experience this psychosomatic principle central to Johnson's imagination. One afternoon several years ago I had gone to the library between classes. I found the books I needed, and as they were being checked out, it began to rain. By the time I arrived at the back door of the library, the sprinkle was a downpour. Hatless, coatless, with no umbrella, and a load of books, I was two blocks from the English Department with five minutes to get to class. I stood in the doorway for a moment trying to decide whether being late or getting soaked was preferable. Meanwhile, a young man with an umbrella had come up beside me. Thinking he might be headed my way, I asked, "Are you going to the Arts and Science Building?" "Yes," he answered, opening the umbrella and stepping slightly to one side to shelter me and my books. We walked the two blocks quickly, neither of us completely protected but I more than he. We entered the doorway, and I heard him say goodbye as he turned to walk back down the street. Clearly he had not been coming to the Arts and Science Building. But so instantaneously had he sized up the situation (a person with no coat, loaded down with books, looking perplexed, 2:35 P.M., and so forth) that he had said "Yes" to my question without pause. He made no point of being gallant, no point of going out of his way or doing a favor. He simply gave what was, in terms of the situation as he assessed it, the right answer, though by other criteria not the true one, and then provided the appropriate action. The event gave proof that this person, whose name I never knew, was organized.

The episode is small, one might even say trivial. Certainly the elements are ordinary. But the service performed was real, imaginative, and strategically useful. This manner of thinking gives evidence of a manner and degree of attention to the probable meaning of details in the system of another person's life that is an instance of genius operating in the everyday. This person's imagining was an accurate fiction of the kind Johnson identifies in his praise of the kindness of Richard Savage's jailer—kindness that circumstance, habit, and conventional self-centeredness all mitigate against. Such episodes exemplify a kind of perception, comprehension, communication, and action without which life would be seriously diminished. They embody a pragmatically ingenious manner of thinking that, cumulatively through days, weeks, months, and finally over the years, accounts, by its presence or absence, for the psychological ease or dis-ease, the moral organization or disorganization of our lives. Most notably in the *Rambler* Johnson highlights the importance of such behavior and the kind of thinking that directs it to imagine other people's lives. From these essays alone one could predict that he would have seen the meaning of that student's action as not merely polite but crucial for living, indeed as being as necessary for us to perform for others as to benefit from receiving. From the Johnson who states simply and emphatically that it is "our first duty to serve society, and, after we have done that, we may attend wholly to the salvation of our own souls,"[9] I learned to recognize such acts, to see them as evidence of a healthy imagination at work upon ordinary materials to make a true difference in how we live.

To argue that Johnson "thought biography" offers ways of considering anew some familiar ideas about this writer. Here lies its value for us as readers. From this perspective we may come to see in some new ways why this man has proved over time to be such a compelling teacher yet one whose styles of writing and thinking cannot be imitated literally with any success. To be a Johnsonian, by which I do not mean exclusively to be an academic, has meant for many people the experience of a profound kind of difference he makes in their lives. While he is not unique among authors in making such a difference, his force has proved to be unusually strong and distinctive in its effects. To read him over time is usually to come to see and to think in a family of ways we call *Johnsonian.* Yet his style cannot be imitated in any precise or literal way without the imitator's falling into inadvertent parody. His work resists such false flattery. Being near proof against dishonesty toward ourselves, his writing demands our taking the trouble of converting his style into our own. In the various ways Johnson teaches us, he both requires and empowers our converting that education into something characteristically for and of ourselves, something that, if we happen to be academics, we discover both to come from and go well beyond the printed page of our own work. A consideration of why this happens and how, while not the major aim of this study, has been one of its significant corollaries.

A century and a half after Johnson, Gertrude Stein argued a case

9. Boswell, *Life*, 2:10.

for the indispensable value of genuine repetition, by which she means thoughts repeated by a living mind, as being significantly more creative and original than the merely new.[10] Furthermore, she argues, a narrative of genuine repetition constitutes a biography of mind, the most pleasurable and useful of all stories.[11] Inventing an image to characterize the mind of genius, Johnson similarly proposes that genuine repetition constitutes true pleasure: "He only is the master who keeps the mind in pleasing captivity; whose pages are perused with eagerness, and in hope of new pleasure are perused again; and whose conclusion is perceived with an eye of sorrow, such as the traveller casts upon departing day" (LP 1:454). This passage with its figure of pleasing captivity opens out onto his hope for ongoing education throughout life, the theme in his life and writings most clearly at the center of his biographical thinking. Learning cannot occur without pleasure to motivate it. For Johnson the hope for continued learning centers on associating both learning and teaching with our entire beings. It is a hope, too, for the way repetition and return, those movements necessary for establishing the varied rhythms of true education, which Nietzsche was to make his own at the end of the nineteenth century, are distinct from the mere repetitiousness characterizing education gone wrong.

Another of Stein's insights into this crucial distinction between true and false repetition also sheds light on Johnson. In *Everybody's Autobiography* she gives the name of *school* to education that mistakenly emphasizes learning by rote and the mastering of inert facts. For Johnson, too, such mistaken ideas about learning are dangerous not just to the individuals they miseducate but to an entire culture whom they misdirect in imaginative, ethical, and intellectual matters. Alert to the dangers of false repetition, he also affirmed the epistemological paradox that books, like the world, answer only those questions to which in some sense the answer is already known. Without this foreknowledge, the right answer could

10. Stein discusses these ideas throughout her works, but perhaps most succinctly in "A Transatlantic Interview 1946," 33.

11. The idea of repetition figures centrally in Stein's work, but especially in *The Geographical History of America or The Relation of Human Nature to the Human Mind*. It follows from these remarks about repetition that this study is perhaps better understood to be *of* rather than merely *about* Samuel Johnson. Joel Weinsheimer's *Imitation* offers a stimulating exploration and enactment of this distinction.

never be recognized when it appears. Questions and answers have a complex interwoven chronology. They do not occur along a straight, forward-moving time line. To learn is to recognize and to repeat what one already somehow knows. The new is always a version of the old, the old of the new. Thus the teachers and books that teach us best, like the life best lived, hold us in voluntary thrall to the promise of a newness as familiar as it is refreshing. Unlike those lessons learned from Rasselas's first teacher, which must be forgotten in order to give pleasure, true learning is repeatedly and variously interesting. This notion intersects with the possibility of constructing a present accurately and innovatively connected with the past, as well as imaginatively directed toward our future. Such connectedness is, for Johnson, the precondition for creating that most imaginary, elusive, and essential mode of time, the present.

If for him the experience of pleasing captivity in reading is a paradigm of all successful education, it is also his figure for a life well lived. Pleasing captivity assumes a stance of questioning faith with regard to books and to the world. It is a stance that values our forging, both individually and collectively, an active connection between past and future. Perhaps more importantly, this stance encourages our cultivating a healthy resilience toward, even an anticipation of, pleasure from the experience of differing from others or disagreeing with ourselves over time. Returning to old texts, one finds new pleasures and instruction there and thus learns the useful art differing from oneself. Such differing has intellectual, ethical, and emotional dimensions and values. It provides the opportunity to encounter our mutual differences with relative safety. The importance of this exercise lies in the fact that, as Johnson knew so well and as Woolf brilliantly elaborated in our century, we are generally frightened of difference, which is to say, frightened of one another, "of criticism, of laughter, of people who think differently."[12] Differing from others almost invariably inspires fear, suspicion, and anger. By mock-encountering with our own differences over time in the drama of our pleasing captivity to literature, we experience difference with relative safety. This practice, in turn, provides a solid groundwork for expecting the best, rather than the worst, from our mutual differences. We may thereby perhaps come

12. *The Years*, 414.

to accept those differences charitably and to use them well in the collective conversation of history.[13]

In his *Life of Sir Thomas Browne* Johnson raises an issue that elegantly summarizes the agenda that has guided my study. He notes how Browne failed to write an account of his early travels and regrets how this failure deprived readers of what would have been, almost certainly, a fascinating book. He comments further that those who, like Browne, are most gifted often decide not to write, either because they prefer to collect knowledge than to impart it or because they find few things "of so much importance as to deserve the notice of the publick."[14] Writers of the first kind defer publication for the pleasure of collecting. By this deferral they overemphasize the self and underemphasize the social act of writing. Writers of the second kind defer publication out of a paralyzing sense of humility, underemphasizing the self and the social act of writing. Neither motive is a positive or intended evil. Both, ironically, mark the energetic mind of genius that demands more of itself than it does of others. But in each instance the writer produces nothing. Hence the present, by being left empty, is negated. This negation marks the fact that a serious error has occurred in biographical thinking. Both instances are grave liabilities for the drama of collective creative effort constituting the history of our education.

The empty present is for Johnson the type of all moral and philosophical error. While it may seem philosophically high-minded, as in the case of Browne's decision, to make such a choice, it is, Johnson argues, generally a mistake. Like shyness, this refusal presumes too much self-importance. It fails to conceive the self to be chiefly an agent of work in the world and furthermore to be one among many such agents. By healthy contrast there exist the counteracting attitudes of mind and readiness of imagination to think probabilistically ("We know somewhat, and we imagine the rest," LP 1:235) that typify biography.[15] The problem-solving activity of biographical probability is our fundamental imaginative act, the model of creativity and originality in the Johnsonian sense of origi-

---

13. For a book-length exploration of conversation as one of the possible aims of knowledge, see Rorty's *Philosophy and the Mirror of Nature*. See also Burke's conception of inheritance in *Attitudes toward History*, 125.

14. *Early Biographical Writings of Dr. Johnson*, 417.

15. For a discussion of the proof of probability in the ethos of eighteenth-century literature, see Hoyt Trowbridge's "Scattered Atoms of Probability."

nality defined by James Engell: "Originality now meant the ability to reflect the inner drama and process of a mind charged with feeling as it descries the value and the elusive truths of experience."[16] This ability is not exhausted, indeed it is even enriched, by the activity of repetition. Accurately directed by probability, biography helps us overcome the temptation of neglecting our duty to join in the conversation of history and by this successful participation to fill the present usefully.

Johnson understood and used probability as he understood and used biography. As biography was for him more than merely a kind of writing so, too, probability was more than merely a method or technique of thought. He considered both to be conditions of thinking, models of communication, and ways of living. One might even say that for him probability thinks us and biography lives us. Both provide a motive and model for placing something in the empty present, thereby to assert the meaning that, in turn, makes us. This assertion of meaning is fundamentally constitutive of being. Thus empowered, we find ourselves able to make the psychologically difficult shift from the pleasures of collecting knowledge to the risky, but necessary and responsible, activity of distributing our knowledge according to the rhythms of repetition and recommencement constitutive of true education.

Repetition, as subject, rhythm, and style, which is to say as the character or ethos of Johnson's thinking, finds later expression in the work of Søren Kierkegaard. In turn, Kierkegaard modifies and refines our understanding of Johnson, when he proposes that the question of repetition will play a crucial role in modern philosophy:

> Just as they taught that all knowing is a recollecting, modern philosophy will teach that all life is a repetition. . . . Repetition and recollection are the same movement, except in opposite directions, for what is recollected has been, is repeated backward, whereas genuine repetition is recollected forward. Repetition, therefore, if it is possible, makes a person happy, whereas recollection makes him unhappy. . . . Recollection is a discarded garment that does not fit, however beautiful it is, for one has outgrown it. Repetition is an indestructible garment that fits closely and tenderly, neither binds nor sags. . . . It takes youthfulness to hope, youthfulness to recollect, but it takes courage to will repetition. . . . For hope is a beckoning fruit that does not satisfy . . . but repetition is the daily bread that satisfies with blessing. . . . The person who has not circumnavigated life before beginning to live will

16. "Johnson on Novelty and Originality," 279.

never live; the person who circumnavigated it but became satiated had a poor constitution; the person who chose repetition—he lives.[17]

These remarks recall Johnson's thinking in the way they plot out the simple but demanding task of living, taking into account both its losses and its gains. So, too, in their simple statement of mysterious trust Kierkegaard's insights are reminiscent of his predecessor's thinking on the ideas that have been the chief subjects of my inquiry, namely how living and repetition are one and the same and how "thinking biography" is central to each.

The presuppositions, both substantive and methodological, of my work have, no doubt, been apparent throughout. But it may be appropriate to conclude by stating them explicitly. First, I believe that Johnson is accurate in his opinion that we all take interest in how our own and other people's minds work. This curiosity is an existential urge and a profoundly important one. In attempting to imagine how his mind worked, this study uses Johnson's own inquiries into the creative process as its model. Thus it aims to contribute toward an understanding of the contours of his ways of thinking and to sketch, at least in profile, the rich quality of his intellect and imagination. Second, I assume that a legitimate critical method, as well as an aim of criticism, is moral or ethical. On this point all criticism (deconstruction, new historicism, gender studies, feminisms, formalist criticism, psychoanalysis, Marxism, and so on), though in different styles and by different methods, agrees. Each of these methods differs from the others principally in the way it makes its case for being more genuinely ethical, useful, true, than all the rest. I assume that one of the chief functions of criticism, as of literature, is to teach and by teaching to address one of our strongest urges: the urge to learn, to understand, to acquaint ourselves with the unfamiliar, the urge of simple, life-sustaining curiosity. My critical language is grounded in this conception of criticism as an ethical activity whose chief responsibility is to identify how the meaning of so-called past literature is its value and function in the present, as it applies in complex but nonetheless direct ways to life in the present. Meaning is a verb in the present tense. Finally, I assume that originality in criticism, as in literature, is identical with genuine repetition.

My sentiments on these issues and the critical routes that follow from them are neither fancy nor complicated in and of them-

17. *Fear and Trembling; Repetition,* 131, 132.

selves. Yet neither are they unallied with theory or merely old-fashioned. At best I hope to have combined the practical and the theoretical to give some new views of a familiar Johnson. Writing was for him no special province but rather a name for one of the ways in which we engage with life. As such, his writing invites readers to renew acquaintance not only with his mind and life but also, through his mediation, with our own.

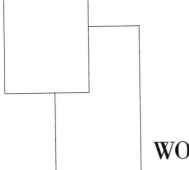

WORKS CITED

Alkon, Paul K. "Johnson and Chronology." In *Greene Centennial Studies: Essays Presented to Donald Greene in the Centennial Year of the University of Southern California*, edited by Paul J. Korshin and Robert R. Allen, 143–71. Charlottesville: University Press of Virginia, 1984.

———. *Samuel Johnson and Moral Discipline*. Evanston, Ill.: Northwestern University Press, 1967.

Bachelard, Gaston. *The Philosophy of No: A Philosophy of the New Scientific Mind*. Translated by G. C. Waterston. New York: Orion Press, 1968.

Balderston, Katherine C. "Dr. Johnson and William Law." *PMLA* 75, no. 4, pt. 1 (September 1960): 382–94.

Basney, Lionel T. "'Ah ha!—Sam Johnson!—I see thee!': Johnson's Ironic Roles." *South Atlantic Quarterly* 75, no. 2 (Spring 1976): 198–211.

Bate, Walter Jackson. *The Achievement of Samuel Johnson*. New York: Oxford University Press, 1955.

———. "Johnson and Satire Manqué." In *Eighteenth-Century Studies in Honor of Donald E. Hyde*, edited by W. H. Bond, 145–60. New York: Grolier Club, 1970.

———. *Samuel Johnson*. New York: Harcourt Brace Jovanovich, 1977.

Bateson, Gregory. *Steps to an Ecology of Mind: A Revolutionary Approach to Man's Understanding of Himself*. New York: Ballantine Books, 1972.

Becker, Carl L. "Everyman his own Historian." *American Historical Review* 37, no. 2 (January 1932): 221–36.

———. "A New Philosophy of History." Review of *The Interpretation of History* by L. Cecil Jane. *The Dial* 59 (1915): 146–48.

————. *"What Is the Good of History?" Selected Letters of Carl L. Becker, 1900–1945.* Edited with an introduction by Michael Kammen. Ithaca: Cornell University Press, 1973.

Bogel, Fredric V. "The Rhetoric of Substantiality: Johnson and the Later Eighteenth Century." *Eighteenth-Century Studies* 12, no. 4 (Summer 1979): 457–80.

Bok, Sissela. *Lying: Moral Choice in Public and Private Life.* New York: Pantheon Books, 1978.

Booth, Mark W. "Johnson's Critical Judgments in the *Lives of the Poets." Studies in English Literature, 1500–1900* 16, no. 3 (Summer 1976): 505–15.

Borges, Jorge Luis. "Nathaniel Hawthorne." In *Other Inquisitions 1937–1952,* translated by Ruth L. C. Simms, introduction by James E. Irby, 47–65. Austin: University of Texas Press, 1964.

Boswell, James. *Boswell's Life of Johnson.* Edited by G. B. Hill; revised and enlarged by L. F. Powell, 6 vols. Oxford: Clarendon Press, 1934–1964.

Boulding, Kenneth E. *The Image: Knowledge in Life and Society.* Ann Arbor: University of Michigan Press, 1956.

Braudy, Leo. "Lexicography and Biography in the *Preface* to Johnson's *Dictionary." Studies in English Literature, 1500–1900* 10, no. 3 (Summer 1970): 551–56.

Burke, Kenneth. *Attitudes toward History.* 1937. 2d ed., rev. Boston: Beacon Press, 1961.

————. *Permanence and Change: An Anatomy of Purpose.* 1935. 2d ed., rev. Los Altos, Calif.: Hermes Publications, 1954.

————. *The Philosophy of Literary Form: Studies in Symbolic Action.* 1941. 3d ed. Berkeley and Los Angeles: University of California Press, 1973.

————. "The Relation between Literature and Science." In *The Writer in a Changing World,* edited by Henry Hart, 158–71. New York: Equinox Cooperative Press, 1937.

Byrd, Max. "Johnson's Spiritual Anxiety." *Modern Philology* 78, no. 4 (May 1981): 368–78.

Clifford, James L. *Dictionary Johnson: Samuel Johnson's Middle Years.* New York: McGraw-Hill, 1979.

————. *Young Sam Johnson.* New York: McGraw-Hill, 1955.

Cockshut, A. O. J. *Truth to Life: The Art of Biography in the Nineteenth Century.* London: Collins, 1974.

Curley, Thomas M. *Samuel Johnson and the Age of Travel.* Athens: University of Georgia Press, 1976.

Damrosch, Leopold J., Jr. "Johnson's Manner of Proceeding in the *Rambler.*" *English Literary History* 40, no. 1 (Spring 1973): 70–89.

———. *Samuel Johnson and the Tragic Sense.* Princeton: Princeton University Press, 1972.

———. *The Uses of Johnson's Criticism.* Charlottesville: University Press of Virginia, 1976.

Davis, Philip. *In Mind of Johnson: A Study of Johnson the Rambler.* Athens: University of Georgia Press, 1989.

DeMaria, Robert, Jr. *Johnson's Dictionary and the Language of Learning.* Chapel Hill: University of North Carolina Press, 1986.

Ellmann, Richard. *Literary Biography: An Inaugural Lecture Delivered Before the University of Oxford on 4 May 1971.* Oxford: Clarendon Press, 1971.

Emerson, Ralph Waldo. "Experience." In *The Complete Works of Ralph Waldo Emerson*, with a biographical introduction and notes by Edward Waldo Emerson, 3:43–86. Centenary Edition, 12 vols. Boston: Houghton Mifflin, 1903–1904.

Engell, James. "Johnson on Novelty and Originality." *Modern Philology* 75, no. 3 (February 1978): 273–79.

Fair, Charles M. *The Dying Self.* Middletown, Conn.: Wesleyan University Press, 1969.

Fitzgerald, F. Scott. *The Crack-Up with Other Uncollected Pieces*, edited by Edmund Wilson. New York: New Directions, 1945.

Fix, Stephen J. "Distant Genius: Johnson and the Art of Milton's Life." *Modern Philology* 81, no. 3 (February 1984): 244–64.

———. "Johnson and the 'Duty' of Reading *Paradise Lost.*" *English Literary History* 52, no. 3 (Fall 1985): 649–71.

Folkenflik, Robert. *Samuel Johnson, Biographer.* Ithaca: Cornell University Press, 1978.

———. "That Man's Scope." In *Samuel Johnson: New Critical Essays*, edited by Isobel Grundy, 31–50. London: Vision Press; Totowa, N.J.: Barnes and Noble, 1984.

Fussell, Paul. *Samuel Johnson and the Life of Writing.* New York: Harcourt Brace Jovanovich, 1971.

Greene, Donald. " 'Logical Structure' in Eighteenth-Century Poetry." *Philological Quarterly* 31, no. 3 (July 1952): 315–36.

Grene, Marjorie. *The Knower and the Known.* Berkeley and Los Angeles: University of California Press, 1974.

Gross, Gloria Sybil. "Sanity, Madness, and the Family in Samuel Johnson's *Rasselas.*" *Psychocultural Review* 1 (1977): 152–59.

Grundy, Isobel. "Samuel Johnson: Man of Maxims?" In *Samuel John-*

son: New Critical Essays, edited by Isobel Grundy, 13–30. London: Vision Press; Totowa, N.J.: Barnes and Noble, 1984.

Hallett, H. F. "Dr. Johnson's Refutation of Bishop Berkeley." *Mind*, n.s., 56, no. 221 (Janaury 1947): 132–47.

Hampl, Patricia. "Surviving a Life in the Present." *New York Times Book Review*, 7 June 1987, 15.

Hart, Francis R. "Johnson as Philosophic Traveler: The Perfecting of an Idea." *English Literary History* 36, no. 4 (December 1969): 679–95.

Hart, Jeffrey. "Some Thoughts on Johnson as Hero." In *Johnsonian Studies*, edited by Magdi Wahba, 23–36. Cairo: Société Orientale de Publicité, 1962.

Hazen, Allen T. *Samuel Johnson's Prefaces and Dedications*. New Haven: Yale University Press, 1937.

Hill, G. B., ed. *Johnsonian Miscellanies*. 2 vols. Oxford: Clarendon Press, 1897.

Hillman, James. *Re-Visioning Psychology*. New York: Harper and Row, 1975.

Holt, John. *How Children Learn*. New York: Pitman Publishing, 1969.

Howard, Donald R. "Lexicography and the Silence of the Past." In *New Aspects of Lexicography: Literary Criticism, Intellectual History, and Social Change*, edited by Howard D. Weinbrot, 3–16. Carbondale: Southern Illinois University Press, 1972.

Irwin, George. *Samuel Johnson: A Personality in Conflict*. Auckland: Auckland University Press, 1971.

James, William. *The Principles of Psychology*. 2 vols. New York: H. Holt, 1890.

Jemielty, Thomas. "Dr. Johnson and the Uses of Travel." *Philological Quarterly* 51, no. 2 (April 1972): 448–59.

———. " 'More in Notions than in Facts': Samuel Johnson's *Journey to the Western Islands*." *Dalhousie Review* 49, no. 3 (Autumn 1969): 319–30.

Johnson, Samuel. *A Dictionary of the English Language*. Facsimile edition. 2 vols. New York: AMS Press, 1967.

———. *Early Biographical Writings of Dr. Johnson*. Edited with an introduction by J. D. Fleeman. Farnborough: Gregg International Publishers, 1973.

———. *The Idler and the Adventurer*. Edited by W. J. Bate, John M. Bullitt, and L. F. Powell. *The Yale Edition of the Works of Samuel Johnson*, vol. 2. New Haven: Yale University Press, 1963.

———. *Johnson on Shakespeare*. Edited by Arthur Sherbo. Introduction by Bertrand H. Bronson. *The Yale Edition of the Works of Samuel Johnson*, vols. 7–8. New Haven: Yale University Press, 1968.

———. *A Journey to the Western Islands.* Edited by Mary Lascelles. *The Yale Edition of the Works of Samuel Johnson,* vol. 9. New Haven: Yale University Press, 1971.

———. *The Letters of Samuel Johnson: With Mrs. Thrale's Genuine Letters to Him.* 3 vols. Collected and edited by R. W. Chapman. Oxford: Clarendon Press, 1952.

———. *Lives of the English Poets.* Edited by G. B. Hill. 3 vols. Oxford: Clarendon Press, 1905.

———. *Poems.* Edited by E. L. McAdam, Jr., with George Milne. *The Yale Edition of the Works of Samuel Johnson,* vol. 6. New Haven: Yale University Press, 1964.

———. *The Rambler.* Edited by W. J. Bate and Albrecht B. Strauss. *The Yale Edition of the Works of Samuel Johnson,* vols. 3–5. New Haven: Yale University Press, 1969.

———. *Rasselas and Other Tales.* Edited by Gwin J. Kolb. *The Yale Edition of the Works of Samuel Johnson,* vol. 16. New Haven: Yale University Press, 1990.

———. *Sermons.* Edited by Jean H. Hagstrum and James Gray. *The Yale Edition of the Works of Samuel Johnson,* vol. 14. New Haven: Yale University Press, 1978.

Kaminski, Thomas. *The Early Career of Samuel Johnson.* New York: Oxford University Press, 1987.

Keast, William R. "Johnson and Intellectual History." In *New Light on Dr. Johnson: Essays on the Occasion of his 250th Birthday,* edited by Frederick W. Hilles, 247–56. New Haven: Yale University Press, 1959. Reprint. Hamden, Conn.: Archon Books, 1967.

———. "Johnson's Criticism of the Metaphysical Poets." Reprinted in *Eighteenth-Century English Literature: Modern Essays in Criticism,* edited by James L. Clifford, 300–310. New York: Oxford University Press, 1959.

———. "The Theoretical Foundations of Johnson's Criticism." In *Critics and Criticism Ancient and Modern,* edited by R. S. Crane et al., 389–407. Chicago: University of Chicago Press, 1952.

Kierkegaard, Søren. *Fear and Trembling; Repetition.* Translated with an introduction and notes by Howard V. Hong and Edna H. Hong. Kirkegaard's Writings 6. Princeton: Princeton University Press, 1983.

Knoblauch, Cyril H. "Coherence Betrayed: Samuel Johnson and the 'Prose of the World.'" *Boundary 2,* "Revisions of the Anglo-American Tradition: Part 1," 7, no. 2 (Winter 1979): 235–60.

Kolb, Gwin J. "'The Vision of Theodore': Genre, Context, Early Reception." In *Johnson and His Age,* edited by James Engell, 107–24. Harvard Studies in English 12. Cambridge: Harvard University Press, 1984.

Korshin, Paul J., ed. *The Age of Johnson: A Scholarly Annual*, vol. 1. New York: AMS Press, 1987.

———. "Johnson's *Rambler* and Its Audiences." In *Essays on the Essay: Redefining the Genre*, edited by Alexander J. Butrym, 92–105. Athens: University of Georgia Press, 1989.

Lascelles, Mary. "*Rasselas* Reconsidered." In *Essays and Studies Collected for the English Association*, edited by Geoffrey Tillotson, n.s., 4, 37–52. London: John Murray, 1951.

Law, William. *A Serious Call to a Devout and Holy Life*, with an introduction by the Very Reverend Norman Sykes. Everyman's Library. 1906. Reprint. London: J. M. Dent and Co., 1967.

Lipking, Lawrence. "Johnson and the Meaning of Life." In *Johnson and His Age*, edited by James Engell, 1–27. Harvard Studies in English 12. Cambridge: Harvard University Press, 1984.

———. "Learning to Read Johnson: *The Vision of Theodore* and *The Vanity of Human Wishes.*" *English Literary History* 43, no. 4 (Winter 1976): 517–37.

Lynch, William F. *Images of Faith: An Exploration of the Ironic Imagination*. Notre Dame: University of Notre Dame Press, 1973.

———. *Images of Hope: Imagination as Healer of the Hopeless*. Baltimore: Helicon Press, 1965.

McIntosh, Carey. *The Choice of Life: Samuel Johnson and the World of Fiction*. New Haven: Yale University Press, 1973.

Maner, Martin. *The Philosophical Biographer: Doubt and Dialectic in Johnson's Lives of the Poets*. Athens: University of Georgia Press, 1988.

Maritain, Jacques. "Art as a Virtue of the Practical Intellect." In *Creative Intuition in Art and Poetry*, 44–70. 3d printing with corrections. Bollingen Series, vol. 35, no. 1. New York: Pantheon Books, 1955.

Marr, George S. *The Periodical Essayists of the Eighteenth Century*. London: James Clarke and Co., 1923.

Merleau-Ponty, Maurice. *Phenomenology of Perception*. Translated by Colin Smith. London: Routledge and Kegan Paul, 1970.

Milner, Marion. *On Not Being Able to Paint*. New York: International Universities Press, 1967.

Nietzsche, Friedrich. *The Use and Abuse of History*. Translated by Adrian Collins, with an introduction by Julius Kraft. 2d ed., rev. Indianapolis: Bobbs-Merrill Educational Publishing, 1957.

Novak, Maximillian E. "Johnson, Dryden, and the Wild Vicissitudes of Taste." In *The Unknown Samuel Johnson*, edited by John J. Burke, Jr., and Donald Kay, 54–75. Madison: University of Wisconsin Press, 1983.

Noxon, James. "Human Nature: General Theory and Individual Lives."

In *Biography in the 18th Century*, edited by J. D. Browning, 8–27. New York: Garland Publishing 1980.

O'Flaherty, Patrick. "Dr. Johnson as Equivocator: The Meaning of *Rasselas.*" *Modern Language Quarterly* 31, no. 2 (June 1970): 195–208.

———. "Johnson in the Hebrides: Philosopher Becalmed." *Studies in Burke and His Time* 13 (1971): 1986–2001.

———. "Towards an Understanding of Johnson's *Rambler.*" *Studies in English Literature, 1500–1900* 18, no. 3 (Summer 1978): 523–36.

Parke, Catherine N. "Imlac and Autobiography." In *Studies in Eighteenth-Century Culture*, edited by Ronald S. Rosbottom, 6:183–98. Madison: University of Wisconsin Press, 1977.

———. "Johnson, Imlac, and Biographical Thinking." In *Domestick Privacies: Samuel Johnson and the Art of Biography*, edited by David G. Wheeler, 85–106. Lexington: University Press of Kentucky, 1987.

———. "Love, Accuracy, and the Power of an Object: Finding the Conclusion in *A Journey to the Western Islands.*" *Biography* 3, no. 2 (Spring 1980): 105–20.

———. "*Rasselas* and the Conversation of History." In *The Age of Johnson: A Scholarly Annual*, edited by Paul J. Korshin, 1:79–109. New York: AMS Press, 1987.

———. "Virginia Woolf: The Biographer as Medium." *Thought* 63, no. 251 (December 1988): 358–77.

Polanyi, Michael. *Personal Knowledge: Towards a Post-Critical Philosophy.* Corrected edition. Chicago: University of Chicago Press, 1962.

Pomponio, Carmen J. "Looking at Johnson's *Life of Dryden.*" *New Rambler*, serial C, 15 (1974): 35–39.

Radner, John B. "The Significance of Johnson's Changing Views of the Hebrides." In *The Unknown Samuel Johnson*, edited by John J. Burke, Jr., and Donald Kay, 131–49. Madison: University of Wisconsin Press, 1983.

Rhodes, Rodman D. "'Idler' No. 24 and Johnson's Epistemology." *Modern Philology* 64, no. 1 (August 1966): 10–21.

Rorty, Richard A. *Philosophy and the Mirror of Nature.* Princeton: Princeton University Press, 1979.

Schwartz, Richard B. "Johnson's 'Vision of Theodore.'" *The New Rambler*, serial C, 14 (Spring 1973): 31–39.

Sherlock, William. *A Practical Discourse Concerning Death.* 19th ed. London: W. Botham, 1723.

Siebert, Donald T., Jr. "Johnson as Satirical Traveler: *A Journey to the Western Islands of Scotland.*" *Tennessee Studies in Literature* 19 (1974): 137–47.

———. "The Scholar as Satirist: Johnson's Edition of Shakespeare." *Studies in English Literature, 1500-1900* 15, no. 3 (Summer 1975): 483-503.

Sledd, James H., and Gwin J. Kolb. *Dr. Johnson's Dictionary: Essays in the Biography of a Book.* Chicago: University of Chicago Press, 1955.

Stauffer, Donald A. *The Art of Biography in Eighteenth Century England.* Princeton: Princeton University Press, 1941.

Stein, Gertrude. *The Geographical History of America or The Relation of Human Nature to the Human Mind.* New York: Random House, 1936.

———. "A Transatlantic Interview 1946." In *A Primer for the Gradual Understanding of Gertrude Stein,* edited by Robert Bartlett Haas, 11-35. Los Angeles: Black Sparrow Press, 1971.

Tillotson, Geoffrey. "Time in *Rasselas.*" In *Bicentenary Essays on Rasselas,* collected by Magdi Wahba, 97-103. Cairo: Société Orientale de Publicité, 1959.

Tomarken, Edward. "A Historico-Literary Text: Samuel Johnson in Scotland." *Eighteenth Century Life* 4, no. 1 (September 1977): 23-28.

———. "Travels into the Unknown: *Rasselas* and *A Journey to the Western Islands of Scotland.*" In *The Unknown Samuel Johnson,* edited by John J. Burke, Jr., and Donald Kay, 150-67. Madison: University of Wisconsin Press, 1983.

Tracy, Clarence, ed. *Life of Savage,* by Samuel Johnson. Oxford: Clarendon Press, 1971.

Trowbridge, Hoyt. "Scattered Atoms of Probability." *Eighteenth-Century Studies* 5, no. 1 (Fall 1971): 1-38.

Vance, John A. *Samuel Johnson and the Sense of History.* Athens: University of Georgia Press, 1984.

Vesterman, William. "Johnson and *The Life of Savage.*" *English Literary History* 36, no. 4 (December 1969): 659-78.

Wain, John. *Samuel Johnson: A Biography.* New York: Viking Press, 1975.

Watt, Ian. "Dr. Johnson and the Literature of Experience." In *Johnsonian Studies,* edited by Magdi Wahba, 15-22. Cairo: Société Orientale de Publicité, 1962.

Weidhorn, Manfred. "The Conversation of Common Sense." *University Review* 34, no. 1 (Autumn 1967): 3-7.

Weinbrot, Howard D. "Samuel Johnson's *Plan* and Preface to the *Dictionary.*" In *New Aspects of Lexicography: Literary Criticism, Intellectual History, and Social Change,* edited by Howard D. Weinbrot, 73-94. Carbondale: Southern Illinois University Press, 1972.

Weinsheimer, Joel. *Imitation*. International Library of Phenomenology and Moral Sciences. London: Routledge and Kegan Paul, 1984.

———. "Writing about Literature and through It." *Boundary 2* 10, no. 3 (Spring 1982): 69–91.

Wheeler, David G., ed. *Domestick Privacies: Samuel Johnson and the Art of Biography*. Lexington: University Press of Kentucky, 1987.

Wimsatt, William K., Jr. "In Praise of *Rasselas:* Four Notes (Converging)." In *Imagined Worlds: Essays on Some English Novels and Novelists in Honour of John Butt*, edited by Maynard Mack and Ian Gregor, 111–36. London: Methuen and Co., 1968.

———. "Johnson's Dictionary." In *New Light on Dr. Johnson*, edited by Frederick W. Hilles, 65–90. New Haven: Yale University Press, 1959.

———. *Philosophic Words: A Study of Style and Meaning in the Rambler and Dictionary of Samuel Johnson*. New Haven: Yale University Press, 1948. Reprint. Hamden, Conn.: Archon Books, 1968.

Wittgenstein, Ludwig. *The Blue and Brown Books: Preliminary Studies for the "Philosophical Investigations."* 1958. Reprint of 2d ed. New York: Harper and Row, 1965.

Woodruff, James F. "Johnson's *Rambler* and Its Contemporary Context." *Bulletin of Research in the Humanities* 85, no. 1 (Spring 1982): 27–64.

Woolf, Virginia. *Collected Essays*. 4 vols. New York: Harcourt, Brace and World, 1967.

———. *The Years*. New York: Harcourt, Brace and Co., 1937.

Wright, John W. "Samuel Johnson and Traditional Methodology." *PMLA* 86, no. 1 (January 1971): 40–50.

INDEX

Addison, Joseph, 55, 56, 70–71, 139, 145; J's life of, 78, 135, 136, 139, 149

Alkon, Paul K., 84

Aristotle, 156

Art of Biography in Eighteenth Century England, The (Stauffer), 1

Ascham, Roger, 11

Bacon, Sir Francis, 64

Baretti, Giuseppe, 28, 36

Basney, Lionel T., 30

Bate, Walter Jackson, 20, 105, 132

Bateson, Gregory, 13, 26, 72, 73

Becker, Carl L., 49, 84, 131, 149–50

Berkeley, Bishop George, 63–64, 72, 110–12

Blackmore, Sir Richard, 148

Bogel, Fredric V., 66–67

Bok, Sissela, 6, 89

Borges, Jorge Luis, 6

Boswell, James, 78–79, 155

Boyle, Robert, 67, 76

Browne, Sir Thomas, 96; J's life of, 94–95, 161

Burke, Kenneth, 6, 77, 78, 82, 151

Butler, Samuel, 141, 142–43, 144

Clifford, James Lowry, 19–20

Cockshut, A. O. J., 133

Congreve, William, 147

Cowley, Abraham, 122; J's life of, 120, 143

Damrosch, Leopold J., Jr., 68, 132

Davis, Philip, 3n4

Denham, John, 136, 148

Descartes, René, 57, 59, 64, 70, 111, 112

Dictionary of Ancient Geography (Macbean): J's preface to, 116

Dodsley, Robert, 9, 12–13, 27

Don Quixote, 60, 66

Dryden, John, 138, 139, 140, 142, 148, 150, 152; J's life of, 49, 138, 140–41, 145, 147, 150, 159

Dying Self, The (Fair), 40–41, 156

Early Career of Samuel Johnson, The (Kaminski), 10n2

Emerson, Ralph Waldo, 5

Engell, James, 162

Essay of Dramatick Poesie (Dryden), 49, 138, 139

Everybody's Autobiography (Stein), 159

Fair, Charles M., 40, 156

Fitzgerald, F. Scott, 107

Folkenflik, Robert, 132

Follett, M. P., 55

Freud, Sigmund, 11

Fussell, Paul, 68

Garrick, David, 9

Gay, John, 148

Goldsmith, Oliver, 58

Gottshalk, Louis, 149
Grene, Marjorie, 59
Grundy, Isobel, 66
Guide Through the Royal Academy
(Baretti), J's introduction to, 28,
36

Hawthorne, Nathaniel, 6
Hegel, George Wilhelm Friedrich,
45
Heidegger, Martin, 84
History of the Royal Society, The
(Sprat), 136–37
Hume, David, 111, 151

"I am Christina Rossetti" (Woolf),
132
Iliad (Pope, translator), 138
*In Mind of Johnson: A Study of John-
son the Rambler* (Davis), 3n4
Irwin, George, 11n4

James, William, 6, 21, 23
Johnson, Elizabeth, 9, 53
Johnson, Samuel: Ideas and Attitudes
—Biography: as way of thinking,
definition of, 1–8, 71, 113, 153–63;
and autobiography, J's distinction
between, 26, 123–24; and the biographer, 131–34, 138
—Critics and criticism, 48–52, 66,
137, 139, 140–41
—Education: threats to, 6–7, 15–19,
25, 94, 101, 115, 149; teaching, J's
early failures in, 9–13, 77–78; role
of habit in, 18, 21–24; role of trust
in, 24, 94; role of acquaintance in,
28, 84–89; threats to and example
of Richard Savage, 112–14
—Genius, 3–5, 39, 49–50, 139,
145–49, 152, 161
—History: as inheritance, 44–45, 74,
134–38; functions of, 80–84, 104,
105–6; conversation as model of,
82–84, 85, 87–89
—Knowledge: role of imagination
in, 3, 6–7, 36, 40, 66–68; causal
and linear thinking, J's dissatisfaction with, 3, 7, 25–26, 27–28,

57, 62–64, 67, 111, 112, 129–30;
as acquaintance, 7, 97–99, 125,
150–51; as personal and interper-
sonal, 18, 28, 43–44, 55, 57, 65,
71–72, 73, 99, 117–18, 152; role of
repetition in, 28–29, 76, 84–86, 88,
158–60, 162–63; hope as structure
of, 40, 115; as curiosity, 47–48,
65–66; and time, 54–55, 59–66;
idealism, J's refutation of, 63–64,
72, 110–12; as intelligibility,
119–22, 125–30
—Lexicography and the lexicographer, 31–43, 45–46, 49–50, 63, 65,
116–17, 128–29. *See also* Johnson:
Writings, *Dictionary* and Preface
to the *Dictionary*
—Prefaces and preface-writing, 7, 8,
28–31. *See also* Johnson: Writings,
Preface to the *Dictionary* and *Preface to Shakespeare*
—Travel writing: as biography, 8,
107–8, 116, 117, 120–24; and education, 114–16, 129–30. *See also*
Johnson: Writings, *A Journey to
the Western Islands of Scotland*
Johnson, Samuel: Writings
—*Adventurer, The*, 53; No. 50, 96
—Biographies (miscellaneous):
"Ascham," 11; "Browne," 94–95,
161
—*Dictionary*, 31–34 *passim*, 93; and
Rambler, 7, 53–54, 56–57, 62; *Plan*
of, 30; and *A Journey to the West-
ern Islands*, 116–17, 129
—*History of Rasselas, Prince of
Abissinia, The. See Rasselas*
—*Idler, The*, 53; No. 44, 115
—Introductions and prefaces (mis-
cellaneous): to Baretti's *Guide
Through the Royal Academy*, 28,
36; to Macbean's *Dictionary of
Ancient Geography*, 116
—*Irene*, 77–79
—*Journey to the Western Islands of
Scotland, A*, 7–8, 51, 107–30, 131,
145; and *Dictionary*, 116–17, 129;
accurate information, problem of
obtaining, 119–23
—*Lives of the English Poets*, 8, 35,

49, 51, 54, 103, 131–52; model of
creativity in, 139, 142, 147, 150;
"Addison," 78, 135, 136, 139, 149;
"Blackmore," 148; "Butler," 141,
142–43, 144; "Congreve," 147;
"Cowley," 120, 143; "Denham,"
136, 148; "Dryden," 49, 138,
140–41, 145, 147, 150, 159; "Gay,"
148; "Halifax," 140; "Milton,"
149; "Pope," 135–36, 140, 145–46,
148; "Roscommon," 3, 161; "Savage," 112–14, 139, 153; "Smith,"
134; "Sprat," 136–37; "Watts," 107
—London, 5
—Prefaces, Biographical and Critical, to the Works of the English
Poets. See Lives of the English
Poets
—Preface to Shakespeare, 7, 29,
43–52, 136, 153; and inheritance,
44–45; on critics and criticism,
48–52
—Preface to the Dictionary, 4, 7, 29,
31–43, 49–50, 54, 133; J's personae
in, 30, 31–36, 44–45, 116; role of
acquaintance in, 36–40
—Preface to The Preceptor, 6–7, 9,
12, 15–19, 24–27 passim, 43, 74,
107; threats to learning in, 15–19
—Rambler, The, 7, 53–76, 113, 158;
and Dictionary, 7, 53–54, 56–57,
62; and time, 54–55, 59–66, 69;
persona in, 55–59, 60; No. 1,
57–58, 60; No. 2, 59–60, 102, 104;
No. 3, 78; No. 4, 92; No. 5, 68;
No. 8, 110; No. 9, 105; No. 17, 62;
No. 25, 63; No. 28, 58; No. 70, 68,
71; No. 79, 68; No. 87, 11; No. 99,
68, 69–70; No. 103, 65–66; No.
106, 67; No. 127, 73–74; No. 129,
75; No. 160, 73; No. 173, 69; No.
208, 72–73
—Rasselas, 7, 34, 39–40, 68, 70,
74–75, 78–106, 114, 117, 120, 131,
141; conversation, importance of,
7, 82–83, 84–89, 91–100, 101–2,
120, 138; boredom, psychology of,
34, 79–84, 86, 88, 105; family life,
debate on, 96–99
—Sermons: No. 3, 24; No. 8, 15; No.

15, 108, 134; No. 18, 23–24; No.
24, 108
—Vanity of Human Wishes, The, 5,
74–75, 142, 143–44
—Vision of Theodore, The, 6–7, 9,
12, 15, 18, 19–26, 27, 74, 107; J's
preference for, 12, 19–20; allegory
of habits in, 21–24
Juvenal, Decimus Junius, 5

Kafka, Franz, 6
Kaminski, Thomas, 10n2
Keast, William R., 132
Kierkegaard, Søren, 162–63
Knoblauch, Cyril H., 35

Law, William, 14–15, 26, 109
Lipking, Lawrence, 19–20
"Lives of the Obscure" (Woolf), 133
Locke, John, 57, 64, 128

Macbean, Alexander, 116
Martial, Marcus Valerius, 76
Martin, Martin (Scots historian),
121–23, 146
Merleau-Ponty, Maurice, 117
Metaphysical poets and poetry, 120,
122, 136, 143
Milton, John, 148, 149, 152
Montaigne, Michel Eyquem de, 57,
122–23

Newton, Sir Isaac, 72
Nietzsche, Friedrich Wilhelm,
159

O'Flaherty, Patrick, 68–69

Polanyi, Michael, 13, 152
Pomfret, John, 142
Pope, Alexander, 135–36, 138–39,
140, 142, 148–49; J's life of,
135–36, 140, 145–46, 148
Practical Discourse Concerning
Death, A (Sherlock), 108–9
Preceptor, The (Dodsley, editor), 9,
27

Raleigh, Sir Walter, 3
Rape of the Lock, The (Pope), 145

Reynolds, Sir Joshua, 29
Russell, Bertrand, 6, 14

Samuel Johnson: A Personality in Conflict (Irwin), 11n4
Santayana, George, 131
Savage, Richard, 112–14, 139, 153
Schwartz, Richard B., 19
Serious Call to a Devout and Holy Life, A (Law), 14–15
Seward, William, 61
Shakespeare, William, 3–4, 46, 47, 49–52 *passim*, 66, 137, 153
Sherlock, William, 108–9
Spectator, The (Addison and Steele), 55, 70–71
Sprat, Thomas, 136–37
Stauffer, Donald A., 1
Steele, Richard, 55, 56, 70–71, 139
Stein, Gertrude, 6, 158–59
Strachey, Lytton, 151
Sutherland, James, 141

Swift, Jonathan, 37, 42, 105

Tatler, The (Addison and Steele), 55, 70–71
"Theoretical Foundations of Johnson's Criticism, The" (Keast), 132
Thrale, Henry, 9
Thrale, Hester Lynch, 9, 61, 155
"Towards an Understanding of Johnson's *Rambler*" (O'Flaherty), 68, 69

Voltaire, François Marie Arouet de, 147

Wain, John, 132
Walmsley, Gilbert, 134
Watt, Ian, 10
Watts, Isaac, 107
Weinbrot, Howard D., 30
Wittgenstein, Ludwig, 6, 123, 128
Woolf, Virginia, 6, 64,132–34, 160